HowExpert Guide to Knitting Socks

101 Tips to Learn How to Knit Socks and Become Better at Sock Knitting

HowExpert with Jeanne Torrey

For more tips related to this topic, visit HowExpert.com/knittingsocks.

Recommended Resources

- HowExpert.com – Quick 'How To' Guides on All Topics from A to Z by Everyday Experts.
- HowExpert.com/free – Free HowExpert Email Newsletter.
- HowExpert.com/books – HowExpert Books
- HowExpert.com/courses – HowExpert Courses
- HowExpert.com/clothing – HowExpert Clothing
- HowExpert.com/membership – HowExpert Membership Site
- HowExpert.com/affiliates – HowExpert Affiliate Program
- HowExpert.com/jobs – HowExpert Jobs
- HowExpert.com/writers – Write About Your #1 Passion/Knowledge/Expertise & Become a HowExpert Author.
- HowExpert.com/resources – Additional HowExpert Recommended Resources
- YouTube.com/HowExpert – Subscribe to HowExpert YouTube.
- Instagram.com/HowExpert – Follow HowExpert on Instagram.
- Facebook.com/HowExpert – Follow HowExpert on Facebook.

Publisher's Foreword

Dear HowExpert Reader,

HowExpert publishes quick 'how to' guides on all topics from A to Z by everyday experts.

At HowExpert, our mission is to discover, empower, and maximize everyday people's talents to ultimately make a positive impact in the world for all topics from A to Z...one everyday expert at a time!

All of our HowExpert guides are written by everyday people just like you and me, who have a passion, knowledge, and expertise for a specific topic.

We take great pride in selecting everyday experts who have a passion, real-life experience in a topic, and excellent writing skills to teach you about the topic you are also passionate about and eager to learn.

We hope you get a lot of value from our HowExpert guides, and it can make a positive impact on your life in some way. All of our readers, including you, help us continue living our mission of positively impacting the world for all spheres of influences from A to Z.

If you enjoyed one of our HowExpert guides, then please take a moment to send us your feedback from wherever you got this book.

Thank you, and we wish you all the best in all aspects of life.

Sincerely,

BJ Min
Founder & Publisher of HowExpert
HowExpert.com

PS...If you are also interested in becoming a HowExpert author, then please visit our website at HowExpert.com/writers. Thank you & again, all the best!

Table of Contents

Introduction: Anatomy of a Sock

Many knitters, from beginners to advanced, are intimidated by the idea of knitting socks. However, most sock patterns do not require any additional or special knitting skills. Socks are one of the more forgiving projects in hiding mistakes because they are worn inside of shoes! This book aims to break down the sock knitting process into manageable sections and provide knitters of all experience levels with confidence in their ability to knit socks.

Tip #1: Grab a sock you already own and try to identify the different parts! It is easier than you may realize!

Before heading straight into the Cast-On, it is imperative to know how socks are structured, how to choose a pattern that matches skill level, how to choose appropriate yarn for the design, and how to choose suitable needles for the thread. This guide does assume some basic knitting knowledge; however, explanations and resources will be given whenever possible to ensure no knitter is left behind. Additionally, a glossary of terms and abbreviations is available at the end of this book. Socks are made up of four to six different parts, depending on the pattern. These sections, listed in order of discussion, are Toe, Foot, Gusset, Heel, Leg, and Cuff.

Throughout this book, the different sock sections will be color-coded for simple identification in the example images.

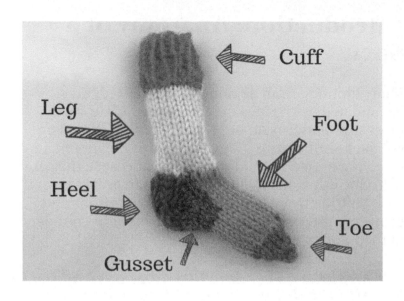

Chapter 1: Choosing Your Knitting Method

Tip #2: Your gauge is a combination of the yarn tension—how tight you hold it—and the needle size.

The most crucial piece of information about knitting socks is there is no one right way to knit socks. If a method or pattern is frustrating, it is perfectly acceptable to modify or scrap it altogether. Slogging through a project that is not enjoyable will undoubtedly be a source of frustration. Finding a comfortable, pleasant method of sock knitting will ensure that the project is fun and relaxing. The most efficient way to determine which method is most comfortable is to do a swatch.

A swatch is a small piece of fabric that is knitted either with the type of chosen yarn, in a portion of the selected pattern, using the intended method, check gauge or any combination of the above. Swatching allows the knitter to practice ahead of time without wasting yarn, as well as to check the gauge of their stitches. The knitting community has complicated feelings concerning doing swatches. Many knitters prefer to jump right into their project and adjust as they knit, forgoing the swatch entirely to save time and yarn. Other knitters will faithfully make swatches for nearly all their projects, betting that their extra time spent now will save them a headache later in the project.

Tip #3: A swatch can be knitted in the round or flat.

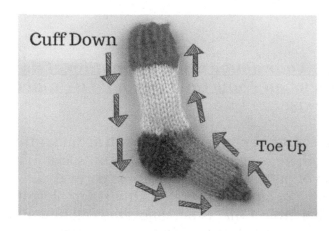

The two most common methods of sock construction are Toe-Up and Cuff-Down in the round—which means the socks are knit as tubes on either Double Pointed Needles (DPNs) or Circular Needles. The name of the method refers to which direction on the sock the sections are knit. Depending on the method chosen, specific construction techniques may need to be adjusted. A gusset on the sole of the sock might be used while knitting from the toe-up, for instance, or the gusset may be omitted altogether if an afterthought-heel is used. Frequently, sock patterns will mention which direction they will be knit. Other knitters will utilize this information to determine whether they want to use a specific design or find a different one. Some pattern designers will include instructions for knitting the socks both toe-up and cuff-down to appeal to a broader array of knitters.

Tip #4: If you are undecided which direction to knit, try knitting a double-sided hexagon! This quick and fun knit gives you an idea of how to work the toe of a sock from both directions.

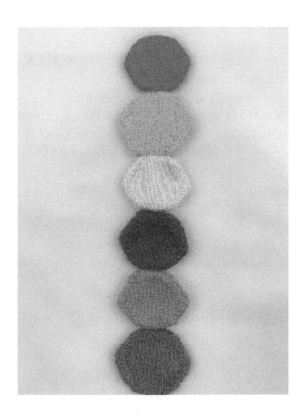

Quick Double-Sided Hexagon Pattern

Abbreviations:
CO – Cast-on
K – Knit

Sts - Stitches
M1R – Make 1 Right
M1L – Make 1 Left
SSK – Slip slip knit
K2TOG – Knit 2 together

1. CO 10 stitches using Judy's Magic Cast-on*.
2. Side 1 – K1, M1R, K to last 2 sts, M1L, K.
3. Side 2 – Repeat Side 1.
4. K across both sides for one round.
5. Repeat Steps 2-4 until there are 20 sts on each needle (40 sts total), ending with a Knit round.
6. Side 1 – K1, SSK, K to last 3 sts, K2TOG, K1.
7. Side 2 – Repeat Side 1.
8. K across both sides for one round.
9. Repeat Steps 6-8 until there are 10 sts on each needle, ending with a Knit round.
10. Cut the yarn leaving a 5-6-inch tail.
11. Use the Kitchener Stitch to seam the remaining sts with the tail.

*If unfamiliar with Judy's Magic Cast-On, it will be discussed later in Chapter 5.

Tip #3: Some knitters dislike seaming with the Kitchener Stitch; if this is the case, try a Three Needle Bind Off for a more traditional line across the toes.

Knitting Socks Using the Toe-Up Method

The toe-up method of sock knitting lends itself more readily to knitting both socks at one time. Fewer stitches are required for the cast to improve needle placement, whether working on two socks or just one. This method can be tricky on DPNs, however. Even though twisting the stitches is less of an issue in toe-up, the DPNs have less physical flexibility than circular needles. The first few rounds of toe-up socks on DPNs can be challenging to maneuver and may cause extra strain on the hands.

Tip #4: The longer the cable in your circular needles, the easier it will be to manage Magic Loop!

The Magic Loop technique, discussed in more depth later in Chapter 2, is a more straightforward way to cast-on and knit socks from the toe-up. The flexible cable gives the knitter additional range on their needles to reach the stitches without any extra effort. It is due to the long cable being pulled through the stitches that are not being worked and freeing up the second needle to work the next set of stitches.

Additionally, when knitting from the toe-up, the heel of the sock is a factor for consideration. An afterthought heel or short-row heel can be incorporated impeccably with minimal effort. However, if a knitter chooses a traditional heel flap, the gusset will need to be adjusted during the toe-up construction. Usually, if a pattern is written toe-up with a heel flap, the gusset will vary on either a double gusset or a riverbed gusset. These types of gussets increase the stitch count on the sole prior to the heel turn, a series of decreases and short rows, before moving onto the heel flap itself. There are some instances when it is preferable to have the gusset located on the sole, such as in colorwork or striped socks, where gusset increases may disrupt the design.

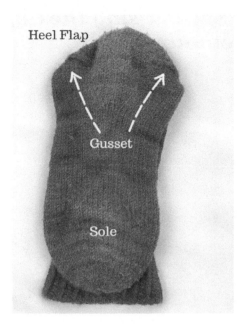

Heel Flap

Gusset

Sole

Pros of Knitting Socks Toe-Up

- Fewer stitches to cast-on
- No toe seaming required

Cons of Knitting Socks Toe-Up

- Knitting a standard heel flap and gusset requires modification
- Initial rounds of knitting are challenging with DPNs

Knitting Socks Using the Cuff-Down Method

Frequently, beginner sock patterns will use the cuff-down method. Both the cuff and leg of the sock are more likely to contain stitches that a beginning knitter will be familiar with, namely knit stitches and purl stitches. There are no increases or decreases, usually, until the knitter gets past the leg and into the heel. The extra time spent on the leg can help the knitter become comfortable knitting a tube in the round. By the time the knitter has reached the heel, they have already been knitting for several inches and will likely have the confidence and excitement to move on to the next stage. The most challenging part of beginning a sock with a cuff-down is stitches can twist around the needles easily, especially on DPNs. Twisted stitches in the round create an infinity-loop effect that is often desirable for scarves but not for socks. "Be careful not to twist" is a frequent note in cuff-down sock patterns for a good reason. Once the first few nerve-wracking rounds on the cuff are completed, it is smooth knitting all the way down to the heel.

Tip #5: Using circular needles to cast-on will minimize the risk of twisting cuff stitches!

Pros of Knitting Socks Cuff-Down

- More patterns are written for knitting cuff-down
- The longest section (leg) finishes sooner

Cons of Knitting Socks Cuff-Down

- More stitches to cast-on
- Stitches can twist more easily

Knitting Socks Using the Two At A Time (TAAT) Method

Second Sock Syndrome is a nickname affectionately used in the knitting community to refer to the procrastination between finishing one sock and finishing the second sock in the pair. It can also refer to the feeling of dread at the thought of repeating something that was just completed again. One of the ways that clever knitters have gotten around Second Sock Syndrome is by knitting both of their socks simultaneously. It is known as Two At A Time (TAAT), and it can look intimidating, especially for beginners.

Tip #6: Infant or child-sized socks are an excellent way to practice knitting TAAT!

Generally, knitting TAAT is done on the same set of long circular needles or using two sets of circular needles. Another method would be using two sets of needles, either circular needles or DPNs or even a combination of the two, with one sock on each set. This method is less common, however. Knitters who prefer two sets of needles will typically knit several rounds on one sock, switch to the other needles, and get caught up on the second sock. If knitting two socks on a single set of needles is daunting but Second Sock Syndrome needs to be avoided, using two separate sets of needles might be the happy medium.

Tip #7: Many knitters prefer to use yarn bowls to help manage yarn. If none are available, standard kitchen bowls can work almost as well!

Pros of TAAT

- Both socks are identical in length
- Finish both socks at the same time
- Stripes and patterns start in the same place

Cons of TAAT

- It takes longer to notice the progression
- Working yarn can get tangled
- It may be more difficult to correct mistakes

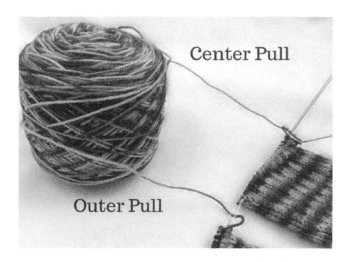

Center Pull

Outer Pull

Yarn management is crucial to using the TAAT method effectively. First, switching strands of working yarn between socks is essential; otherwise, both socks will be knit together into one sock blob. Second, tangled yarn makes knitting TAAT less efficient, it can affect gauge, and it gets frustrating quickly. Some knitters prefer to split their yarn into two balls, allowing them to keep each strand of working yarn physically separate from the other. Others will wind their yarn into a center-pull cake and use both ends of the yarn, one end for each sock. Knitting two socks from one cake do require some extra diligence, specifically in flipping the cake over to the non-center-pull side while knitting from the outer edge. Flipping the cake ensures that the yarn coming from the outer edge does not wrap around the yarn coming from the center. It takes a little extra practice and patience, but it is more space-efficient than two separate balls of yarn.

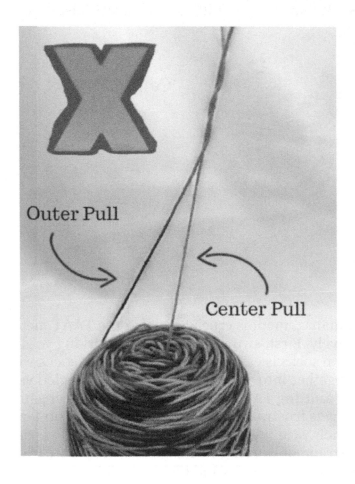

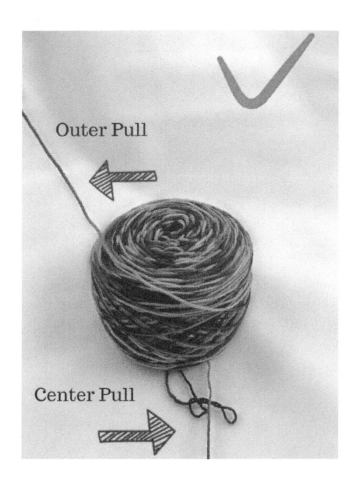

Outer Pull

Center Pull

Knitting two socks at once can be done either toe-up or cuff-down; however, the cast-on will be different. On one set of long circular needles using Judy's Magic Cast-on for toe-up, it is simple enough to cast-on one sock and then the other. However, when using one set of needles and knitting cuff-down, the cast-on strategy must be adjusted. The most straightforward approach would be to follow these steps:

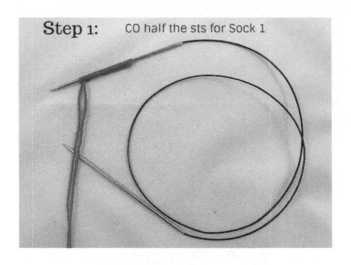

Step 1: CO half the sts for Sock 1

Step 1: Using the desired method, cast on half the necessary number of stitches for the first sock.

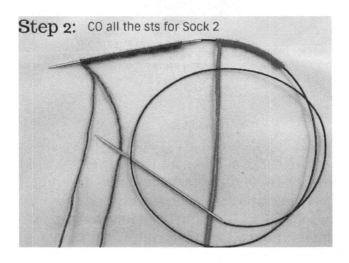

Step 2: CO all the sts for Sock 2

Step 2: With the second strand of yarn, cast on all the necessary stitches for the second sock.

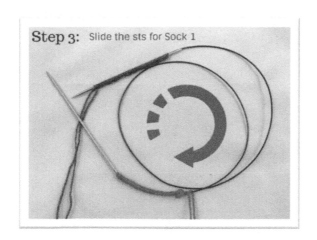

Step 3: Slide the sts for Sock 1

Step 3: Slide both sets of stitches onto the cable of the circular needles.

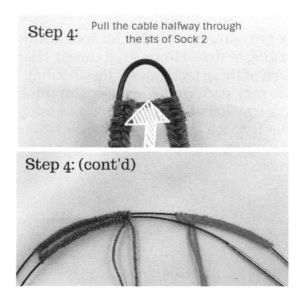

Step 4: Pull the cable halfway through the sts of Sock 2

Step 4: (cont'd)

Step 4: Locate the middle of the second sock's stitches and pull the cable through, splitting the stitches in half.

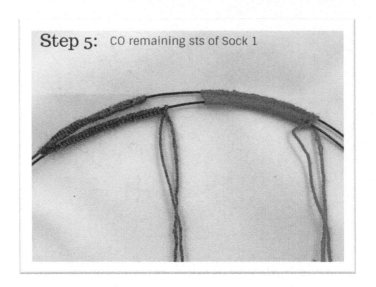

Step 5: CO remaining sts of Sock 1

Step 5: Cast-on the remaining stitches of the first sock.

The number of options available for sock knitting can be intimidating at first. However, if time is taken to practice each of these techniques, they become easier to recognize in sock patterns. The important thing is determining which method is most fun, comfortable, and efficient for each knitter. Socks are an immensely rewarding knitting project, and they will last for many years to come.

Tip #8: Binding off both socks from the toe-up will follow nearly the same format as casting on the cuff.

Chapter Review

- Knitting socks Toe-Up means fewer stitches to cast-on and no toe seaming required
- The Toe-Up method also requires a standard heel flap, and the gusset requires modification
- More patterns are written for knitting socks Cuff-Down
- The longest section (leg) is finished sooner while knitting Cuff-Down
- Both socks are identical in length when knitted Two At A Time (TAAT) and completed at the same time
- Knitting socks TAAT may make it more difficult to correct mistakes, and yarn can tangle easily

Chapter 2: Choosing Your Needles for Knitting Socks

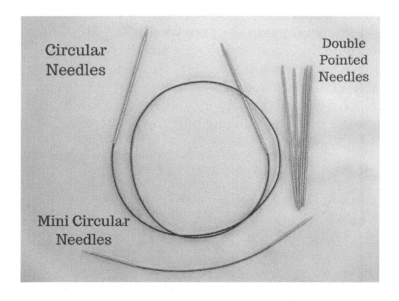

Knitting needles come in all sizes, lengths, materials, colors, and even shapes. Bamboo needles are suitable for knitters who want to keep their stitches from slipping too easily, while metal needles allow knitters to slide their stitches smoothly along. Wooden needles warm quickly to the knitter's touch, and acrylic needles have a slight, but still noticeable, flexibility under tension. While the material of a pair of knitting needles does affect a knitter's gauge, the most significant influence on the gauge is the needles' size.

Tip #9: Many Local Yarn Shops (LYS) have needles available to try before buying.

A swatch is the best way to determine whether a knitter has the appropriately sized needles for their yarn choice. Depending on the yarn weight, explained in more detail in Chapter 3, needle size can cause the gauge to vary by a wide margin. The visual difference between US size 0 and US size 8 needles may seem slight, a mere three millimeters, but it means the difference between a strong fabric and holey socks.

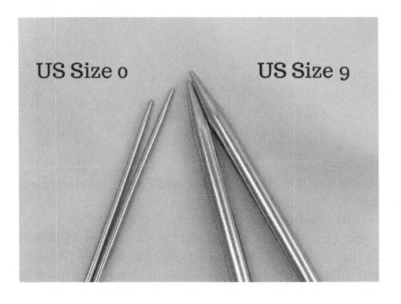

The tighter the gauge, the better it is for sock knitting. The closer the stitches are to each other, the stronger the fabric. It is the reason that most socks are knit in fingering weight yarn. With more stitches per inch, the material that is created is denser and able better to tolerate the friction of day-to-day wear. It is common to see patterns call for US size 0-2 needles for fingering weight yarns to achieve the necessary gauge.

Tip #12: You can use your finger/nail to check the gauge of your swatch or sock. If you press into the fabric, do the stitches hold tight, or do they stretch open too much?

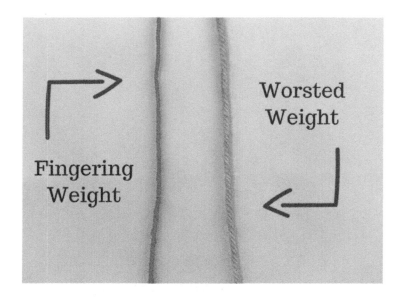

Worsted weight socks, however, are a favorite for sock beginners. Worsted yarn is a medium weight that can still provide a dense enough fabric for socks even at US size 6-8. The thicker material allows knitters to see progress more quickly and reduce the number of stitches needed for both the socks' length and width. Worsted weight yarn is less likely to come in a hearty nylon blend; something knitters should keep in mind when considering what size yarn to choose.

Double Pointed Needles

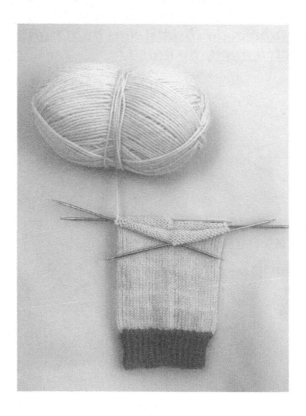

Tip #10: Stoppers on straight knitting needles are a relatively new idea and were not documented until the early 1800s.

Most people are familiar with traditional, straight-knitting needles. They are long, usually metal or bamboo, with tapered points and stoppers to keep stitches from sliding off the backs. To the outsider, working Double Pointed Needles (DPNs) appears daunting. As their name states, DPNs have two points per needle, one on each end, with the intent of allowing stitches to slip off the back. Sets of four to five DPNs enable knitters to create narrow tubes of knitting seamlessly, which is ideal for socks. The work can also be knitted back and forth on DPNs for techniques such as heel flaps or short rows.

Tip #11: DPNs were created in the Middle East during the 12th century B.C. and spread worldwide via trading routes.

A concern when using DPNs, aside from the standard "being careful not to twist" notation, is laddering. Laddering occurs in knitting when the space between stitches—typically between the last stitch on one needle and the first stitch of the next needle—is too loose and resembles the rungs of a ladder.

To avoid laddering while knitting on DPNs, the knitter should take care to knit the first three to four stitches of a needle slightly tighter than usual. The tension of any given knitted stitch is affected by the tension of the stitches around it, which is why simply pulling the first stitch tighter on a DPN is not always sufficient to avoid laddering.

Pros of Using Double Pointed Needles

- Smooth transition between each needle
- Compact and easily transported

<u>Cons of Using Double Pointed Needles</u>

- Stitches can twist and go unnoticed during cast-on
- Laddering can occur in more locations

Magic Loop with Circular Needles

Circular needles, also called cable needles, first made their appearance at the turn of the 20th century. The sturdy cord between two needles allowed knitters not only to work on larger single projects, such as blankets, but they also offered an alternative to DPNs for knitting in the round. The newest advancement in knitting technology since the addition of stoppers on the backs of straight needles, circular needles provided a level of improvement to sock and sweater knitting that is still seen today.

Tip #12: Prior to the invention of circular needles, knitters used long DPNs to create large pieces.

Magic Loop utilizes a long circular needle where knitters cast on the desired number of stitches then pull the excess cable halfway through, which creates the appearance of "loops" on each side of the work. Instead of knitting in the round over three to four needles or "sides," Magic Loop allows knitters to work in the round on only two needles by keeping the stitches not currently being worked on the cable.

Tip #13: Magic Loop was created by Sarah Hauschka and first documented in the 2002 book The Magic Loop by Beverly Galeskas.

A single loop variation on the Magic Loop technique is known as the Traveling Loop. This method can be utilized if the cable on a pair of circular needles is not long enough to pull through for two loops. In this way, the knitter can pull the cable through at the beginning of a round to create the loop, knit the full round, then at the beginning of the next round, repeat the same steps.

Pros of Using Magic/Traveling Loop

- Needles are connected, less likely to get dropped or lost
- Laddering easier to avoid

Cons of Using Magic/Traveling Loop

- The cable can become kinked or get in the way
- Bulkier than DPNs for transport

Short Circular Needles

Fewer tools in the knitting community are as polarizing as the short, or mini, circular needles. The shortest standard circular needle measures 16 inches in length from tip to tip. The shorter-than-standard circular needles measure from 9-12 inches in length and are very much a specialized tool. These needles allow knitters to work socks, sleeves, baby hats, or mittens in the round without fiddling with DPNs or Magic Loop.

Tip #14: Because these needles are not standard, they may be difficult to find in a chain store. The internet is the best place to look!

Many knitters with a dislike for DPNs or using Magic Loop find the short circular needles to be "life changing." However, this is not always the case for every knitter with aversions to a type of needle. The defining characteristic of whether a knitter will love or hate these needles seems to be where they typically hold their needles. Besides the shorter cable between needles, the length of the needles themselves is also decreased from the standard. A knitter whose hands usually hold and maneuver the needles with their fingers closer to the points may have less difficulty adjusting to the mini needles. In contrast, a knitter who relies heavily on their palm or ridge to manipulate the needles and stitches may have trouble shifting their method to their fingers.

Ergonomics may seem like a relatively minor consideration while choosing knitting tools, and if one is knitting for a half hour or less, it might not be an issue. Some knitters will sit down and knit for hours at a time, or whose job it is to knit, and in those instances, good ergonomics are crucial. Injuries can be sustained while knitting, either immediate injuries or over the long term, such as carpal tunnel syndrome. In many cases, they could be avoided with the correct tools. Unfortunately, the only way to know whether short circular needles are an appropriate choice for a knitter is to test them.

Tip #15: You may be able to find a local or online knitting group willing to lend their mini circular needles for a test run.

Pros of Using Short Circular Needles

- Ability to knit continuously without adjusting multiple needles or loops
- Laddering is not an issue

Cons of Using Short Circular Needles

- A short needle may require different hand placement
- Not versatile for non-sock projects

Ultimately, knitters are not restricted to any one method of knitting socks. Perhaps one knitter prefers short circular needles for everything except toe decreases and switches to DPNs. Another knitter may use DPNs until they get to the heel and switch to Magic Loop. Still, another might prefer Magic Loop for knitting TAAT and DPNs for solo sock stitching. Working up a swatch not only provides information on a knitter's gauge and what size needles to use, but it is also an opportunity to try a new method and evaluate the knitter's comfort level with it. In the case of short circular needles, a tubular swatch is also a possibility, especially with scrap yarn if the purpose of the swatch is to try the needles.

Tip #16: Online tutorial videos are another way that knitters learn and share information with each other.

There are many tools available to help knitters of all abilities and methods. The best way for a knitter to see what works is to try different things until one feels comfortable or enjoyable. If metal needles cause stitches to drop, bamboo provides additional friction. If wooden needles are too brittle and metal needles are too cold, acrylic needles offer strength and flexibility.

Chapter Review

- Needle material can impact gauge and comfort
- DPNs allow for a smooth transition between each needle
- Projects are more compact and easily transported on DPNs
- Magic Loop method means needles are less likely to get dropped or lost
- Laddering is easier to avoid using Magic Loop
- Short circular needles allow for continuous knitting
- Laddering can be avoided altogether utilizing short circular needles

Chapter 3: Choosing Your Sock Yarn

Choosing yarn may be the single most exhilarating experience for knitters, second only to binding off a long-term project. Each new ball, skein, or hank of thread holds within its coils endless possibilities. Walking down the yarn aisle of a craft store or across the threshold of a yarn shop can feel as though the morning sun has dawned on a brand-new day. Anything can happen.

Tip #17: If you haven't shopped for thread in person before, don't worry, it's ok to touch, squeeze, pet, and hold just about everything!

In much the same way that choosing the right needles will impact how enjoyable a project can be, correctly selecting the right yarn is also a factor in project pleasure.

Thread can be made up of different fibers, naturally occurring or artificial, plant or animal. It can also be made up of several plies or a single-ply; the weight or thickness will vary greatly, too. All these elements are jumping-off points; they are not rules written in stone. Knitting socks is best enjoyed when the knitter uses their preferred tools and yarn; there is no wrong way to knit socks. Arm knitting may be the only "wrong" way to knit socks; the thread is too chunky.

Yarn Dye Variations

Variegated yarns are dyed to have a mottled effect. In some cases, the colors are complementary, and others are contrasting. There is not usually a pattern or design, though, depending on gauge, sometimes an effect called "pooling" will occur. Pooling is when the same colors pool together in the same place, row after row. It is preferable to some knitters but undesirable for others; still, others may be project-dependent. Variegated threads are best paired with projects with little-to-no texture in the sock's leg and foot. The variances in the thread's colors will often obscure or completely mask textures more complicated than a wide ribbing. Stockinette and Garter stitches are well suited for variegated yarns.

One way of achieving a variegated look is to apply the dye by hand. Depending on the dyer, hand-painted batches of a particular colorway may be small or large. Knowing how much yarn is needed for a pattern is crucial in this instance as the dye can vary between dye lots.

<u>*Tip #19: The process to dye yarn with plant-based dyes dates back to Asia, roughly 5000 years ago!*</u>

A relative newcomer on the knitting scene is a self-striping yarn. As it is knit up, the thread will slowly stripe itself over several rows—thin or thick stripes will depend on the stitch count and knitter's gauge. There are some independent dyers online and a handful of commercial ones that specialize in self-striping yarn. It is a joy to knit striped socks without having to worry about managing multiple balls of yarn or endlessly sewing in tails for each stripe. The dying process for a self-striping thread is a bit different than other methods. Rather than immersing the entire hank in a commercial vat of dye or laying it out and hand painting, self-striping yarn is wound on a swift or strung onto pegs; then the dye is applied stripe by stripe.

Tip #20: Etsy.com is a great place to start looking for "indie" dyers who sell self-striping yarn.

When the yarn is still in the hank, it is twisted and wrapped in a way that does not easily lend itself to self-striping. By laying the thread out in a more linear way, the dyer can create a pattern that will stripes as the yarn is knit. Much like variegated yarn, self-striping knits up best with minimal texture from the stitches. Stockinette is an excellent choice, although well-placed slip stitches can create a unique blending effect between the stripes.

Another method of dying available to independent dyers is kettle dying. The name is a bit misleading because a large stainless-steel pot is used, not a tea kettle. The dyer will immerse the yarn into a pot of water which is colored by dye, and as the water is heated, the thread will slowly absorb the color pigments. Depending on the type or amount of dye, the yarn could come out variegated or solid utilizing the kettle dye method.

Tip #21: If you'd like to try your hand at dying yarn without breaking the bank, look for "Kool Aid in a Crock Pot" dye instructions. It's easier than you think and smells delicious!

Yarn Fiber Blends

There are many different types of wool from varying breeds of sheep. Two of the most popular types of wool come from the Bluefaced Leicester (or BFL for short) and Merino. BFL originated in the United Kingdom around the 18th century and is prized for its crisp stitch definition. Many knitters appreciate the rustic and hearty feel of a BFL yarn between their fingers. Merino has a much longer history, dating as far back as Morocco in the 12th century, and has been bred with a luscious softness still highly sought after today. Merino yarns are ideal for projects being worn close to the skin; it's even suitable for baby garments.

Tip #22: Fiber types are why shopping for yarn in person can be fun; it all feels so different.

When it comes to the yarn being spun explicitly for knitting socks, it is not uncommon to find nylon in with the wool. Nylon provides an added layer of strength to the wool fibers, making the overall yarn more durable and capable of standing up to the friction of being worn inside of shoes. Nylon blends of all types became popular in the early 1950s when textile shops and consumers alike learned that nylon and other fibers were better together. Nylon blends have remained a top choice for sock yarn since then.

Acrylic yarns came onto the knitting scene at roughly the same time nylon blends did. Synthetic fibers from a polymer were cut into staple lengths like wool (staples in wool are the fiber's individual hairs) and from there spun into thread. Despite being first created in the early 1940s, mass production didn't start on acrylic yarn until the 1950s. Suddenly yarn could be produced from start to finish in a factory without having to wait on a raw fleece from sheep. Faster production times led to lower costs to the consumer, which meant knitters could buy more yarn with less money. Yarn stashes everywhere rejoiced. Acrylic yarn does not have the same breathability as wool due to its polymer base and is not recommended for socks.

Tip #23: One of the same companies, DuPont, that worked on the nylon/wool blend also came up with some of the first acrylic yarns.

Other natural fibers that can be blended with wool or spun into yarn on their own include cashmere, alpaca, mohair, silk, cotton, and bamboo. Cotton and bamboo blends could be substituted if wool were to be avoided for socks, especially if there is also nylon in the mix. However, alpaca, mohair, and silk are more delicate fibers on their own and have a more difficult time holding up to the wear and tear socks endure. Cashmere blend yarns are soft and delightful to work with; garments drape beautifully and feel airy next to the skin. A cashmere blend sock yarn is a true splurge for a knitter.

Yarn Weights (Thicknesses)

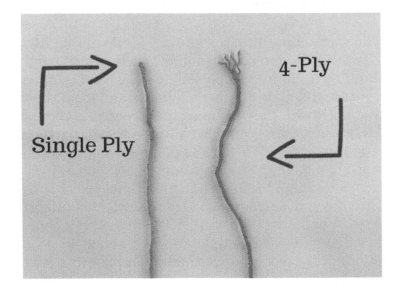

Wool (or other material mentioned above) in its raw form must be spun into yarn. First, the fleece is spun into a single-ply in one direction, and then multiple plies are spun together in the opposite direction to balance the energy infused into the fibers. The thickness of each ply determines the final thickness, or weight, of the finished thread. Some yarns are made from a single ply, and knitters may prefer this for its light and airy feel in finished garments; however, it is not recommended for socks. Multiple plies will make for a stronger yarn, which is necessary for projects that will need to endure significant amounts of friction, such as a sock being worn inside a shoe.

Tip #24: An individual hair that makes up wool is called a "staple."

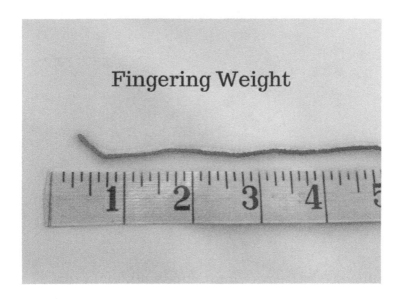

Fingering weight yarn is the most common for knitting socks as it has some of the finest, thinnest plies. The small gauge gives knitters a tighter, stronger fabric that will better withstand friction. Skeins of fingering weight yarn typically come in 400-yard increments, which is more than enough for one pair of adult-sized socks.

Needle sizes US 00 through US 2 are most used to achieve proper gauge with fingering weight yarn.

Tip #28: "Staple length" is sometimes seen when discussing yarn, especially when the subject is spinning yarn. Different breeds of sheep produce wool of varying staple lengths.

Coming in a bit heavier than fingering weight yarn is sport weight yarn. Sport weight is a good choice for knitters whose gauge is already very tight or for knitters who prefer to see their socks progress faster than fingering weight. Because the sport weight is thicker, the needles and stitches will be slightly larger than fingering, helping the knitter achieve more inches with fewer stitches. However, since sport weight is not as common for socks as fingering, there are not always many choices for strong fiber blends in sport weight.

Skeins typically come in 200-yard increments in sport weight, and knitters usually achieve gauge on US 3 through US 5 sized needles. Depending on the pattern, two skeins may be necessary for adult-sized socks.

Tip #29: Cotton has a staple length too, it ranges from 0.39ths of an inch to 2.4 inches.

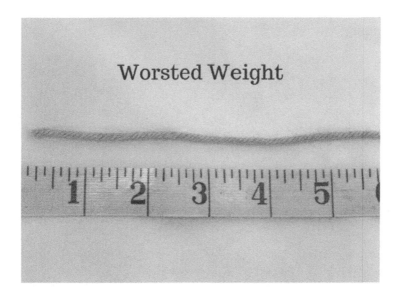

Possibly the single most popular weight of yarn is the worsted weight. This medium-weight thread is incredibly versatile and can be used in everything from socks to sweaters. Worsted weight yarns do not often have nylon blends for socks, but knitters can get around this by using smaller needles to achieve an extremely tight, strong fabric. There are many options of worsted weight yarns on the market to choose from due to their popularity. Worsted is generally the largest weight selection available at chain craft stores, making it one of the easiest to buy. Most skeins come in 200-yard increments, and gauge can be achieved on US 6 through US 9 sized needles. Knitters may need two or more skeins for adult-sized socks.

__Tip #25: Staple length will determine what kind of spinning methods are used to spin the yarn, so the microscopic "scales" on each staple will twist and lock together.__

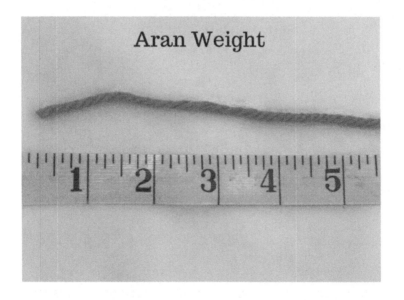

Aran weight yarn falls between worsted and bulky weight. While too bulky to be worn with shoes, socks knit out of Aran weight yarn make for excellent house socks or slippers. The larger weight knits up quickly enough that a pair of socks could be achieved in a matter of days. Knee or thigh-high socks can even be easily knit up in Aran weight yarn, a feat many knitters avoid in fingering weight! Skeins typically come in 100 to 200-yard increments, and gauge is achieved on size US 10 through US 12 needles. A knitter would likely need three or more skeins for adult-sized socks in Aran weight.

Tip #31: The tighter the twist in a yarn as it is made, the stronger that thread will be.

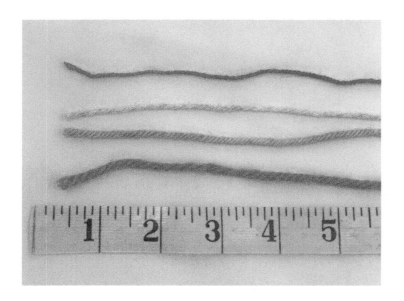

Caring for Yarn by Type

In order to ensure that handknitted socks live their longest and best life, it is imperative to care for them correctly according to the fiber type. As mentioned above, yarns made of a nylon blend will be the strongest and best suited for socks undergoing typical sock wear. That is not to say other blends should be avoided for socks; rather, knitters should consider how often they want to wear the knitted socks, whether the socks will be worn in shoes, and so forth when deciding on the fiber type.

Tip #26: When drying a handknit project, it helps to have a fan circulating air in the room. Bonus if the project can even have air circulate under it!

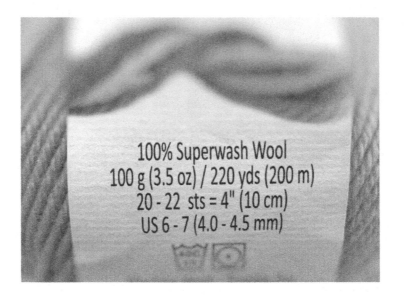

Often, wool is the fiber of choice for sock knitters. Wool will shrink and felt when subjected to hot water and friction, such as in a washing machine. The simplest method to clean wool socks is to hand wash them with mild soap and lay flat or hang dry. Some wool yarns are listed as "Superwash," which means they have been chemically treated to be more resistant to temperature changes and friction. Superwash wools may be a good option if the knitter's socks tend to find their way to a washing machine accidentally. However, the overall process of transforming yarn into Superwash is not considered environmentally friendly due to the harshness of the chemicals used in the process.

Tip #27: If you're still worried about throwing your hand knits in the washing machine, you can still clean Superwash wool projects by hand with mild soap.

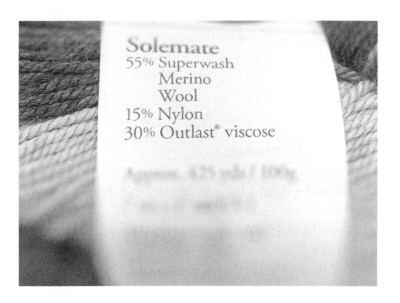

Socks knit with nylon blend yarns should be cleaned with the same level of care as those made of wool; hand wash with mild soap and lie flat or hang dry. The reason for this is nylon blends are precisely that: blends. Most of the fiber in a nylon blend is still wool, about 75% or higher, with nylon covering the remaining 25% of the content, less if there are additional fiber types.

***Tip #28: Many major online yarn retailers
carry special mild soap just for soaking yarn.
Even some of the smaller retailers have this
special soap!***

While not typically used for sock knitting, cotton yarns
are some of the most durable on the market. Projects
knitted with cotton yarn can be repeatedly put through
the washing machine and dryer and come out looking
nearly as good as the day they were bound off. Cotton is
much less forgiving to work with than wool or
wool/nylon blends, with very little ease or stretch;
however, if a pair of socks must absolutely, positively
last a person who is tough on socks, cotton could be the
correct choice.

Chapter Review

- When in doubt how to clean: hand wash and lay
  flat to dry
- Yarn blends with nylon are extraordinarily
  strong
- Avoid acrylic yarn for sock knitting
- Fingering weight: 400yd increments, US 00-2
  needles, one skein per pair of socks
- Sport weight: 200yd increments, US 3-5 needles,
  two skins per pair of socks
- Worsted weight: 200yd increments, US 6-9
  needles, two or more skeins per pair of socks
- Aran weight: 100-200yd increments, US 10-12
  needles, three or more skeins per pair of socks

Chapter 4: Choosing Your Sock Knitting Pattern

What is left to choose for knitting socks once the yarn and needles have been picked? The pattern. Thanks to the World Wide Web, knitting patterns are more accessible than ever, and it is easy to be overwhelmed by the sheer magnitude of available options. Would a hard copy of a design be better than a digital download? Where can a knitter even find a physical pattern book in this digital age? What is a reasonable price for a pattern? Wouldn't a free design be just as good?

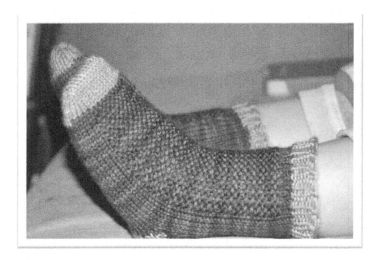

__Tip #29: One of the best examples of a new-to-sock-knitting pattern (it's available for free!) is Rye by TinCanKnits, on their website, www.tincanknits.com/pattern-SC-rye.html__

For those new to knitting in general, the best way to try things out is to work with free patterns. In much the same way, free sock patterns can help a knitter learn whether they actually like knitting socks or not. If there is a designer, dyer, or brand that a knitter particularly enjoys, they may find spending a few dollars on a pattern perfectly acceptable. Supporting other fiber enthusiasts is rarely a bad idea, and the knitting community is full of big hearts worth supporting.

Tip #30: If possible, check to see if other knitters have reviewed or commented on a pattern before buying. It may help you decide on a design or steer clear.

Things to look for regarding a pay-for pattern include clarity, whether it was test knit (which means it is less likely to have typos), does the design include multiple sizes if applicable, and whether charts are included. Professionally written patterns will range from $2 each to $7 or $8, depending on the level of effort. It is not uncommon to find designers who put together an e-book for around $15 for multiple patterns.

Where to Find Sock Patterns

Ravelry.com has been the modern knitter's go-to site since its inception in 2007. All manner of fiber enthusiasts found a place to belong on Ravelry. Designers upload and sell their patterns through Ravelry, knitters (and crocheters) create project pages to track and show off their work, and dyers can market their yarn to a captive audience. The search interface for patterns allows a user to filter results by many options, including the level of difficulty as rated by other crafters. Tantalizing photos of finished projects (FOs) line up in neat rows, enticing the user to pick their pattern.

Another online option for sock patterns is Etsy.com for smaller, independent dyers. Hosting a store is relatively inexpensive for online sellers, which gives potential buyers a wide variety of options they might not typically have. Some sellers may offer kits of both patterns with yarn, physical designs, or instant downloads of PDF files. Kits are especially enjoyable for someone who wants the work of finding a suitable thread for a pattern done for them. It makes the process simple, and many dyers sell kits for this reason.

Tip #31: Spring and Fall are popular seasons for areas to hold sheep and wool festivals. For example, Maryland Sheep & Wool Festival is held in the Spring, and the New York State Sheep & Wool Festival (nicknamed "Rhinebeck" for its host city) is held in the Fall. Festivals are an excellent way to see and feel yarn and patterns "in the wild."

Both commercial yarn brands and independent dyers often host patterns on their websites or provide them in books or kits at craft stores. Many of these patterns will incorporate the brands' or dyers' threads, but if the knitter's gauge aligns with the design, then another yarn brand is perfectly acceptable. Some brands also have free patterns available in the yarn aisles of major craft stores, which is immensely convenient, especially if a knitter does not necessarily have ready access to the internet.

One of the hidden gems for locating sock patterns, or any knitting patterns, is the local library. There are some cases where a design is only offered in an expensive, hardcover book with many other patterns that do not interest the knitter. In this case, a trip to the library may be in order to see if they carry a copy of the book. Often, libraries will also have magazine subscriptions with issues available to check out or photocopy.

Tip # 32: Knitting books will be under 746.43 of the Dewey Decimal System at the library, between architecture and photography.

Types of Knitting Stitches in Patterns

Garter Stitch is what most knitters learn first, and while many are eager to get into more complicated stitch patterns, garter combines an element of texture with ease, unlike most other stitches. The finished result of garter stitch fabric is incredibly stretchy, squishy, and warm. It is a stable stitch that will not roll or curl at the ends of the material and is often used as an edging in patterns for this reason. Knitting in the round, a garter stitch is achieved by alternating knit rounds with purl rounds. If knitting flat (and/or back and forth), only the knit stitch is needed to attain the classic garter ridges.

Knitting Garter Stitch

Flat:
Row 1 (Right Side): Knit all stitches
Row 2 (Wrong Side): Knit all stitches
Repeat

In The Round:
Round 1: Knit all stitches
Round 2: Purl all stitches
Repeat

Tip #39: Garter stitch makes for delightfully squishy heels and toes in socks!

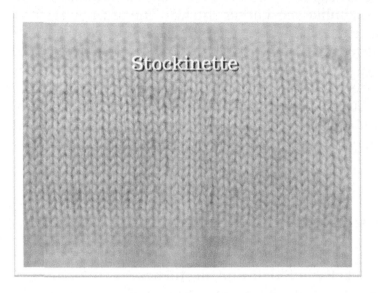

The quintessential knit fabric, with all the "purl bumps" in the back (or wrong side), is known as stockinette stitch. Stockinette provides a finished fabric that is flat on the front, making for nearly seamless stripes. It is stretchy, much like garter stitch, but it does tend to roll at the edges if no other stitches are used to help keep it flat. Stockinette is a favorite for knitters in the round as only the knit stitch is needed, which makes it perfect for "tv knitting" when counting stitches is not necessary. While knitting flat, stockinette is done by knitting on the right-side row and purling on the wrong-side row.

Knitting Stockinette Stitch

<u>Flat:</u>
Row 1 (RS): Knit all stitches
Row 2 (WS): Purl all stitches
Repeat

<u>In The Round:</u>
Round 1: Knit all stitches
Repeat

1 - Left Pattern: Vanilla Bean Striped Socks by Emily O'Grady, Right Pattern: Kick in the Pants by Lollipop Yarn

To new knitters, stripes can seem more complicated than they are, and they are especially fun for socks. At the beginning of a new row or round, to start a stripe, the knitter switches the color of the working yarn and knits with the new color until the line is the desired width. Stripes can be knit either in garter stitch or in stockinette, though it should be noted that the color change in garter should happen on the first of the two rows that make up a ridge. If the color changes on the second row of the garter stitch, the ridge will appear to be split between the two colors, and it does not look as clean a switch between the working yarns. The other thing to consider with striping socks is will the stripes continue through the heels (pictured Right and Bottom) or will a contrasting/complementary color (pictured Left and Top) be used to keep the striping continuous.

Tip #34: Stripes are the oldest textile pattern in history; nobody knows how far back this technique goes!

Knitting Stripes

Garter Stitch (Flat):
Rows 1-6: Knit in Main Color (MC)
Rows 7-12: Knit in Contrast Color (CC)
Repeat Rows 1-12

Garter Stitch (In The Round):
Round 1: Knit in MC
Round 2: Purl in MC
Repeat Rounds 1-2 two more times (six rounds total)
Round 7: Knit in CC
Round 8: Purl in CC
Repeat Rounds 7-8 two more times (six rounds total)
Repeat Rounds 1-12.

Stockinette Stitch (Flat):
Row 1: Knit in MC

Row 2: Purl in MC
Repeat Rows 1-2 two more times (six rows total)
Row 7: Knit in CC
Row 8: Purl in CC
Repeat Rows 7-8 two more times (six rows total)
Repeat Rows 1-12.

Stockinette Stitch (In The Round):
Rounds 1-6: Knit in Main Color (MC)
Rounds 7-12: Knit in Contrast Color (CC)
Repeat Rounds 1-12

Tip #42: If the idea of stripes is still daunting, seek out some self-striping yarn and cast-on with no worries!

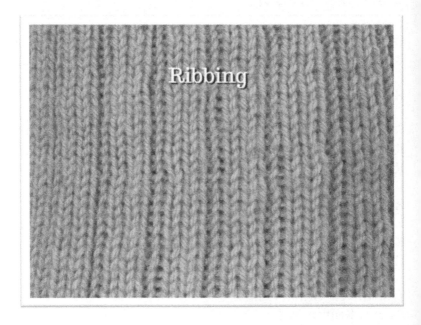

Even non-knitters are familiar with the concept of ribbing, whether they realize it or not. Ribbing, which consists of alternating knits and purls in the same row or round (ex: knit 2, purl 2), has a natural elasticity that makes it an excellent choice for the cuffs of sleeves and socks. It is also reversible, which many knitters like for brims of hats or cuffs on gloves. Ribbing is versatile, simple, and chic. Many sock patterns call for ribbed cuffs as they help the socks stay up on the wearer's leg without falling. Socks themselves can also be ribbed to provide negative ease (the tighter fabric that hugs the body), which allows the sock to fit more snugly on the foot, adding to the sense of security that it is not going to slip down.

Tip #35: The horizontal equivalent of vertical ribbing is known as Welting. Instead of alternating stitches (ex: K2 P2), Welting involves alternating rows (ex: 2 rows knit, 2 rows purl).

Knitting Ribbing

2x2 Rib (Flat or Round):
Cast-on: a multiple of 4 stitches
Row/Round 1: (Knit 2, Purl 2) to end
Repeat Row/Round 1.

3x1 Rib (Flat or Round):
Cast-on: a multiple of 4 stitches.
Row/Round 1: (Knit 3, Purl 1) to end
Repeat Row/Round 1.

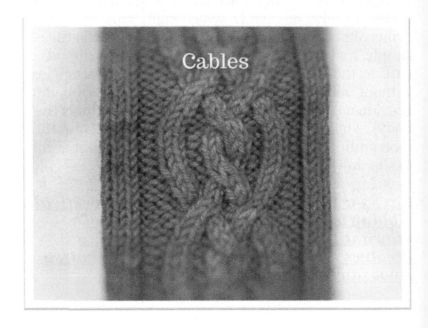

Cables

2 - Pattern: Vancouver Fog by Jen Balfour

Few things are more timeless than a cable-knit sweater. A cable is worked by knitting the stitches in a row out of order, either with a cable needle or using one of several techniques without a cable needle. Cables can vary from simple twists to complicated Celtic knots, and they add a touch of elegance to sock patterns. Because of the way cables create a bulge where the stitch order is changed, they are not recommended on the sock's sole, where they could cause discomfort while walking.

Tip #37: For neater cables, purl the first stitch after a cable through the back loop. It will pull it just a bit tighter, then on the next row or round, purl it as you normally would.

Knitting Cables

Horseshoe Cable (Flat):
Cast-On 18 stitches.
Row 1: Purl 3, Knit 12, Purl 3.
Row 2: Knit 3, Purl 12, Knit 3.
Repeat Rows 1-2 once more (four rows total).
Row 5: Purl 3, slip the next 3 stitches onto a cable needle or stitch holder and hold to the back; Knit 3, Knit the 3 stitches from the cable needle or holder, slide the next 3 stitches onto a cable needle and hold them to the front, Knit 3, Knit the 3 stitches from the cable needle, Purl the last 3 stitches.
Row 6: Knit 3, Purl 12, Knit 3.
Repeat Rows 1-6.

Horseshoe Cable (In The Round):
Cast-On 18 stitches.
Rounds 1-4 and 6: Purl 3, Knit 12, Purl 3.
Round 5: Purl 3, slip the next 3 stitches onto a cable needle or stitch holder and hold to the back; Knit 3, Knit the 3 stitches from the cable needle or holder, slide the next 3 stitches onto a cable needle and hold them to the front, Knit 3, Knit the 3 stitches from the cable needle, Purl the last 3 stitches.

Left Leaning Cable:
Cast-On: 10 stitches, or a multiple of 10 to repeat.

Row 1: Purl 3, Knit 4, Purl 3.
Row 2: Knit 3, Purl 4, Knit 3.
Repeat Rows 1-2 one more time (four total rows).
Row 5: Purl 3, slide the next 2 stitches onto a cable needle and hold them to the front; Knit 2, Knit the 2 stitches from the cable needle, Purl the last 3 stitches.
Row 6: Knit 3, Purl 4, Knit 3.
Repeat Rows 1-6.

Right Leaning Cable:
Cast-On: 10 stitches, or a multiple of 10 to repeat.
Row 1: Purl 3, Knit 4, Purl 3.
Row 2: Knit 3, Purl 4, Knit 3.
Repeat Rows 1-2 one more time (four total rows).
Row 5: Purl 3, slip the next 2 stitches onto a cable needle or stitch holder and hold to the back; Knit 2, Knit the 3 stitches from the cable needle or holder, Purl the last 3 stitches.
Row 6: Knit 3, Purl 4, Knit 3.
Repeat Rows 1-6.

Tip #38: Cables and Celtic knots in knitting are centuries old, potentially dating back to around 800 AD.

Colorwork

3 - Pattern: Nordic Stripes by Tobi Beck

Colorwork has a unique advantage for socks in that carrying multiple strands of yarn over the rounds adds an additional layer to the fabric. This extra layer makes it stronger than it would be on its own, making colorwork an excellent option for socks where a strong material is needed. However, the challenge with colorwork, achieving patterns within the fabric using different colored yarns on socks, is gauge. There is a fine line to walk between a tight enough gauge that enables the various threads to hold the pattern's shape and is so tight that the sock will not fit over a person's heel. Since the foot of the sock does not go over the heel, this section may be tighter in gauge, but it is the leg where the knitter does need to be careful.

Tip #39: Another form of colorwork in knitting is known as Double Knitting, where two (or more!) pieces of fabric are knit simultaneously with two (or more) different yarns.

Knitting Colorwork

Simple Colorwork Pattern (In The Round):
Cast-On: a multiple of 4 stitches in MC.
Round 1: Knit around in MC.
Round 2: (Knit 3 in MC, Knit 1 in CC) around.
Rounds 3-4: Knit around in MC.
Round 5: (Knit 2 in MC, Knit 1 in CC, Knit 1 in MC) around.
Rounds 6-7: Knit around in MC.
Repeat Rounds 1-7.

Lace

4 - Pattern: Skip to My Lou by Rae Jean

Socks are an excellent project to try out lace knitting. Generally, the leg and top of the foot are knit in lace, and the heel, gusset, and sole are typically Stockinette for strength. Having a smaller canvas on which to knit lace gets the knitter through the rounds quickly, and if there are mistakes made along the way, the socks can be hidden in shoes or under pant legs. Some lace patterns lend themselves well in a tubular form on the leg of a sock, while others may only be a small panel running down the front or back of a sock. Lace socks have the opposite problem of colorwork, the gauge is often looser, and socks may slide down more often without a sturdy, ribbed cuff to hold them up.

Tip #41: In 1897, Queen Victoria—an avid Shetland lace knitter—presented abolitionist Harriet Tubman with a lace shawl.

Knitting Lace

Fan and Feather (alternatively "Old Shale," Flat):
Cast-On: 24 stitches or a multiple of 24.
Row 1 (RS): Knit
Row 2 (WS): Purl
Row 3 (RS): *(K2TOG) 4 times, (YO, Knit 1) 8 times, (K2TOG) 4 times. Repeat from * to end.
Row 4 (WS): Purl.
Repeat Rows 1-4.

Fan and Feather (In The Round):
Cast-On: 24 stitches or a multiple of 24.
Rounds 1-2: Knit
Round 3: *(K2TOG) 4 times, (YO, Knit 1) 8 times, (K2TOG) 4 times. Repeat from * to end.
Round 4: Knit
Repeat Rounds 1-4.

Tip #42: An Orenburg Shawl is a traditional Russian knit shawl made with super fine goat yarn. They are also known as "wedding ring shawls" since, despite being quite wide, the work was so fine it could pass entirely through a wedding ring.

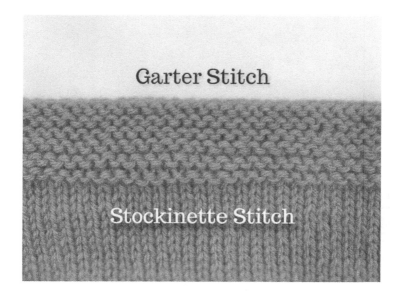

Garter Stitch

Stockinette Stitch

Chapter Review

- Sock patterns can be found online, through yarn dyers/manufacturers, in books, and at the library
- Many free designs are available; however, pay-for patterns may be more thoroughly written or charted
- Sock pattern prices can vary from $2 each to $15 or more for a set

- Ribbing is commonly used in sock cuffs and can also be used throughout the sock itself for a snug fit
- Lace socks are a great way to try lace
- Garter, Stockinette, stripes, and cables are timeless and classic

Chapter 5: Casting On Your Socks

Turkish Cast-on (Toe-Up)

If you need a seamless cast-on for toe-up socks in a hurry, look no further than the Turkish Cast-On. It is just as simple as wrapping yarn around a needle. In fact, it is wrapping the yarn around two needles; then it's over. This cast-on method can leave the original stitches a little loose if not careful to pull tight; however, it is less formidable than Judy's Magic Cast-On for seamless beginners.

Tip #43: The first-ever wool socks discovered by archaeologists were dated to around 100 AD. They were made from a woven cloth for a child.

Setup for Turkish Cast-On: Hold both circular needles together in your left hand and the working yarn in your right hand.

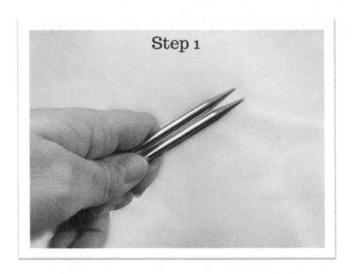

Step 1

Step 1: Hold the yarn's tail firmly under your left thumb, wrap the working yarn around both needles.

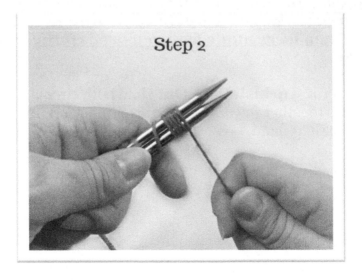

Step 2

Step 2: Repeat Step 1 until **half the number of desired stitches** are cast-on.

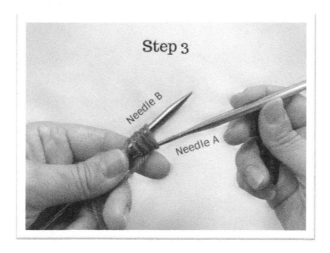

Step 3: Pull the back needle (Needle A) out of the stitches so they are now on the cable, and knit across the front needle (Needle B).

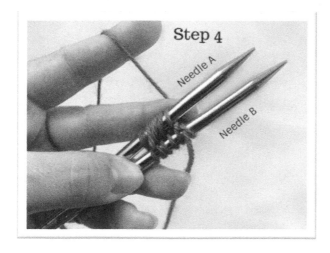

Step 4: Pull Needle B out of the stitches, putting them on the cable, and slide the now-front stitches from the cable to Needle A.

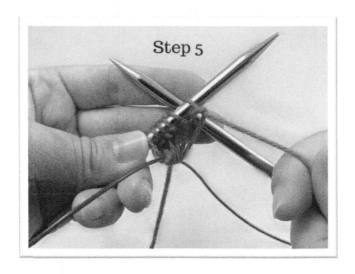

Step 5: **Knit through the back loop** across Needle A.

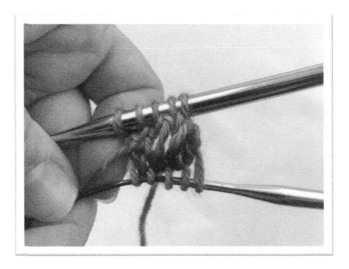

The Turkish Cast-On is now complete, and the toe of your sock(s) is ready for increases!

Judy's Magic Cast-On (Toe-Up)

In the spring of 2006, a new seamless cast-on stunned the knitting world. Judy Becker, a blogger living in Oregon, published steps for a cast-on she developed after growing tired of other common cast-on stitches. While more complicated than the Turkish Cast-On, Judy's Magic Cast-On can be just as fast once the movements are memorized. It also provides a more even tension for the stitches across both needles while having the benefit of a seamless cast-on.

Tip #44: Ancient Egypt is responsible for the first known pairs of knitted socks, from between 300 and 500 AD, which could be worn with sandals thanks to a split-toe design.

Setup for Judy's Magic Cast-On: Using a pair of circular needles, Needle A will be the top needle (furthest away from you), and Needle B will be the bottom needle (closest to you). This cast-on will require the length of the tail as well as the working yarn to add stitches.

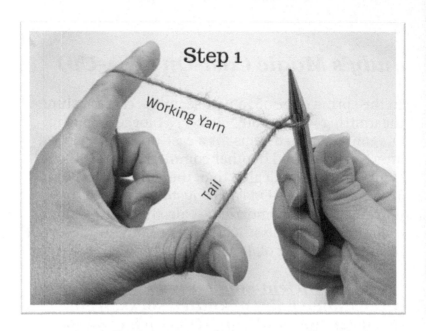

Step 1: Either tie a slip knot or loop the yarn around Needle B so the working yarn is held away from you and the tail is held towards you. This is the first stitch.

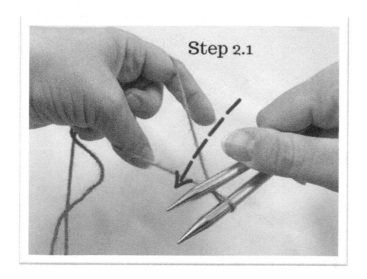

Step 2.1

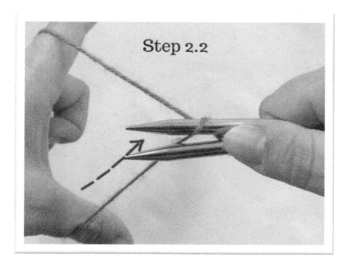

Step 2.2

Step 2: Each needle will loop its opposite yarn. Holding the needles together, swing them down past the tail[2.1] and, using Needle A, loop it underneath[2.2] as you bring the needles back up. Return to the neutral position. There is now one stitch on each needle.

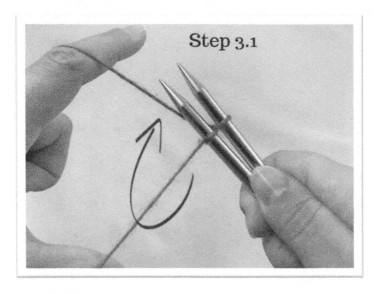

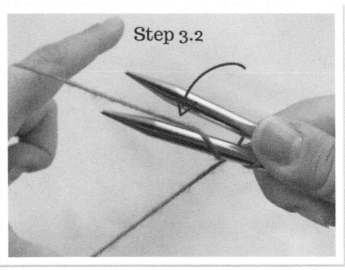

Step 3: Swing both needles up past the working yarn[3.1] and, using Needle B, loop it underneath[3.2] as you did in Step 2. Return to the neutral position.

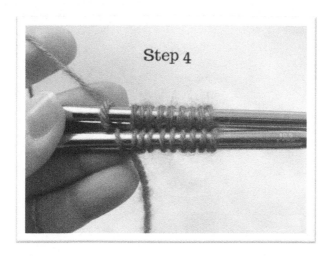

Step 4: Repeat Steps 2 and 3 until you have cast-on as many stitches per needle as needed, ending after a Step 2 stitch.

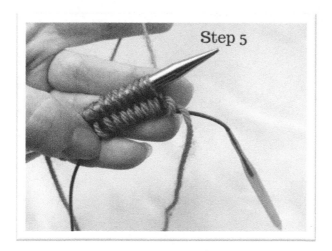

Step 5: Holding the needles in your left hand, ensure the tail down between the needles, pull the back needle out, and knit across the front needle.

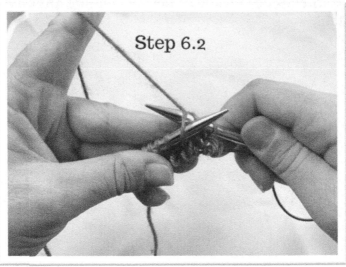

Step 6: The stitches on what is now the front needle are twisted[6.1], **knit through the back loop**[6.2] across the needle to straighten them out.

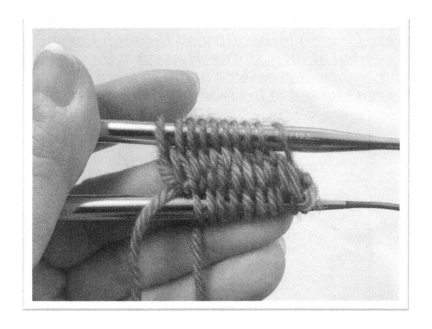

Judy's Magic Cast-On is now complete!

Long Tail Cast-On (Cuff-Down)

The Long Tail Cast-On has a significant benefit of knitting a row of stitches as it goes in addition to being a speedy cast-on. Its name is accurate; you will need a long tail to achieve this cast-on if you want to get it right the first time. There is a relatively easy and fast method to determine how much length your tail will need without a ruler and leaving enough left over to weave in at the end.

<u>Tip #45: By 1000 AD, knit and woven socks were favored by nobility all through Europe as a symbol of their status. However, these socks were more like modern leggings, and feet weren't added to the design until around 1100 AD.</u>

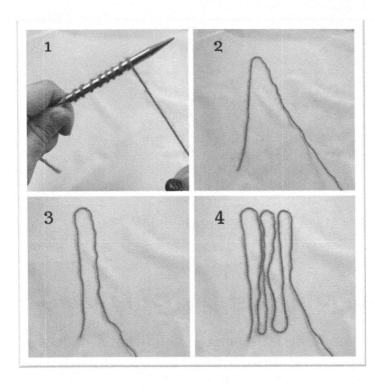

Setup for Long Tail Cast-On: Using either a pair of circular needles or a set of Double Pointed Needles, wrap the yarn around needle[1] ten times. Take the length of thread off the needle[2] and use it to measure more sections of yarn[3] by 10s until you are close to your cast-on number[4].

Step 1: Make a slip knot and place it on one of the needles.

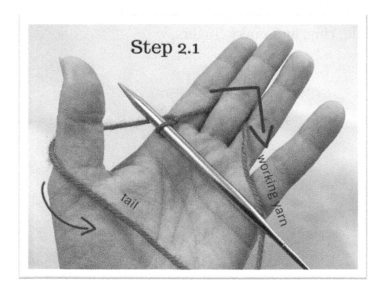

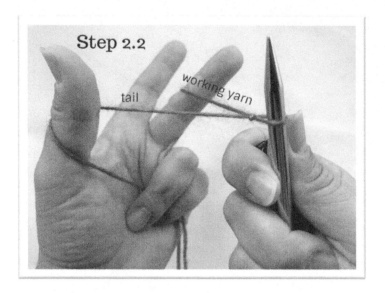

Step 2: Holding the Needle in your right hand, wrap the working yarn around the back of your left index or middle finger and the tail around the back of your thumb. Secure the thread if you can with your left middle, ring, and pinky fingers.

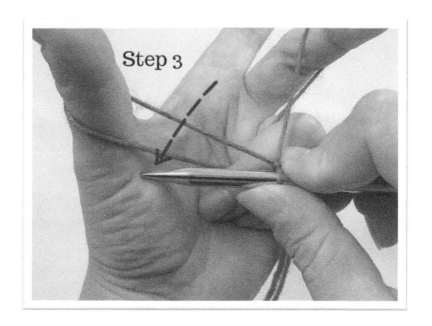

Step 3

Step 3: Bring the Needle down to the outside of the loop on your thumb and bring it under the yarn.

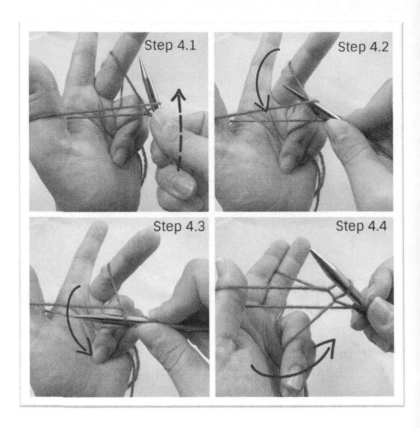

Step 4: Move the Needle up and come around to the outside of the loop on your index or middle finger[4.1]. Bring it down through the loop and catch the inside "leg"[4.2-3], pulling it down between the legs of the loop on your thumb[4.4].

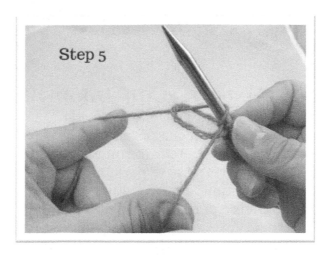

Step 5: Return the Needle to the starting position and use your thumb or right hand to pull the tail (closest to you) tight. There are now two stitches on the Needle.

Step 6: Repeat Steps 1-5 until you have cast-on the desired number of stitches.

The Long Tail Cast-On is now complete!

Knitted Cast-On (Cuff-Down)

The Knitted Cast-On is a classic and with good reason. This cast-on is not as stretchy as some of its counterparts; however, it is remarkably durable and holds up well over time. For well-loved socks, the Knitted Cast-On is a perfect choice.

Tip #46: France and Italy paved the way for silk stockings around 1400 AD, favoring the cool fabric for its weight and flexibility.

Setup for the Knitted Cast-On: This cast-on can be done with either a pair of circular needles or two Double Pointed Needles. The working yarn is held for tension as if you are knitting.

Step 1: Make a slip knot on the Left Needle.

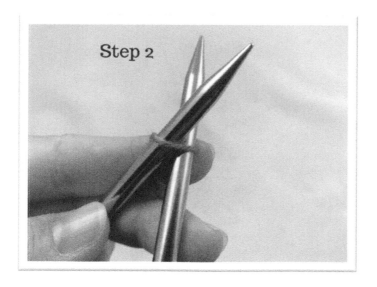

Step 2: Insert the Right Needle through the slip knot, right to left and front to back.

Step 3: Wrap the working yarn around the Right Needle

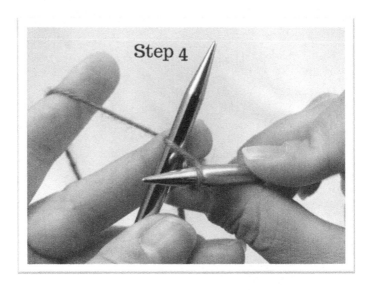

Step 4: Pull the Right Needle back through the slip knot

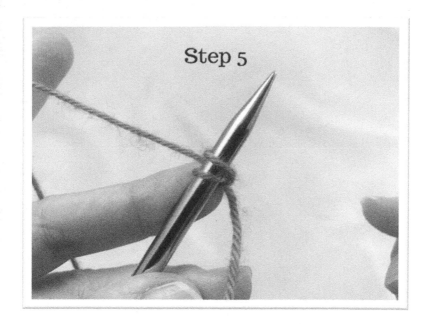

Step 5: Place the loop from the Right Needle onto the Left Needle. There are now two stitches on the Left Needle.

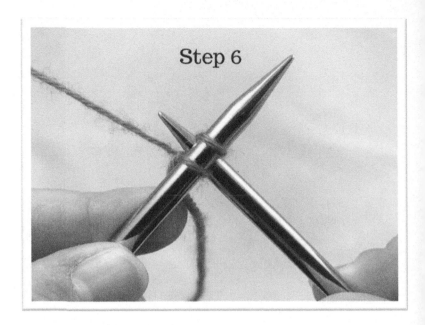

Step 6: Insert the Right Needle between the two stitches on the Left Needle and wrap the working yarn around the needle.

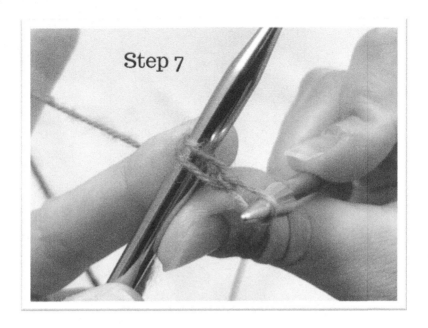

Step 7: Pull the Right Needle back through the stitches and place the loop from the Right Needle onto the Left Needle. There are now three stitches on the Left Needle.

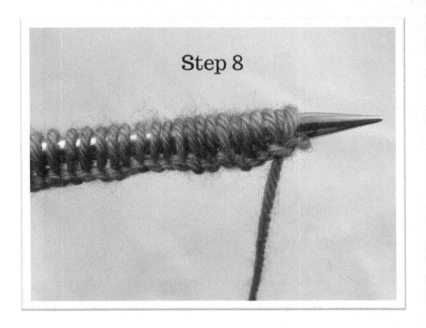

Step 8: Repeat Steps 6 and 7 by inserting the Right Needle between the first and second stitches on the Left Needle until the desired number of stitches has been cast on.

Step 9

Step 9: Distribute the stitches evenly on the remaining needle(s), being careful not to twist.

The Knitted Cast-On is complete!

Chapter Review

- Turkish and Judy's Magic Cast-On are both seamless
- Seamless Cast-On is suitable for the toe-up method
- Long Tail Cast-On knits a row as it is cast-on
- Knitted Cast-On is less stretchy but holds its shape over time

Chapter 6: Knitting the Toe of Your Sock

Determining Increases (Toe-Up) and Decreases (Cuff-Down)

While the example socks in this book make use of the most common toe shape, the wedge, there are many other types of toe options available in patterns. The types of stitches will also influence the fit of the toe, most are knit in stockinette, but some patterns play with the texture of garter stitch, lace, or ribbing. Working in the round requires a pattern designer, or knitter executing a modification to the pattern in their project, to calculate the location of the increases/decreases and the frequency when considering the desired toe shape.

Tip #47: The first knitting machine was invented in 1589 by William Lee in England.

Many sock patterns instruct the knitter to work the foot until it is "about two inches away" from the next desired point (either the heel or toe). In some cases, however, two inches may be too much or not enough. What is a knitter to do in those cases? There is no universal, "one size fits all" measurement for human feet, but there are several good methods to adjust as needed.

Cuff-down socks can be tried on or measured from the heel and compared to a measurement of the intended foot to help ensure the best fit. Many standard toe patterns, especially the wedge, can be used while excluding the pinky toe. It can be considered while knitting cuff-down by working the foot up to the tip of the pinky toe before beginning to work the decreases of the toe box.

Wedge Instructions

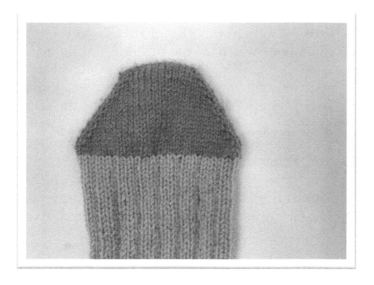

A standard wedge toe will alternate rounds of knitting and increases/decreases. For folks who prefer a wider toe box on a sock, this is often accomplished by more frequent increases/decreases over fewer rows. The result is a wider, shallower toe, for example, two rounds of decreases, then a knit round, and repeating in that three-round pattern. There will also be additional stitches left to graft or cinch to keep the toe's width.

Toe-Up

Step 1: Using your choice of method, cast on the prescribed number of stitches and arrange needles so both halves of the sock are easily identified. Stitch markers are recommended but not necessary.

Step 2: Knit 1 round.

Step 3: Knit 1 stitch, Make 1 Right (M1R), knit to the last stitch before the end of the first half, Make 1 Left (M1L).

Step 4: Repeat Step 3 for the second half of the stitches in the round.

Step 5: Knit 1 round.

Step 6: Repeat Steps 3-5 until the stitch count reaches the desired circumference. Proceed to the foot.

Cuff-Down

Step 1: Ensure the stitches are arranged on the needles, so both halves are easily identified. After completing the foot of the sock, at the beginning of a round, knit 1 stitch, Slip Slip Knit (SSK) decrease, knit to the last 3 stitches, Knit 2 Together (K2TOG), knit the remaining stitch.

Step 2: Repeat Step 1 on the second half of the stitches.

Step 3: Knit 1 round.

Step 4: Repeat Steps 1-3 until about 10-12 stitches are remaining.

Step 5: Graft the toe closed using the desired method.

Tip #48: Queen Elizabeth I did not like the socks produced by Lee's knitting machine, criticizing the scratchy wool.

Pointed Toe Instructions

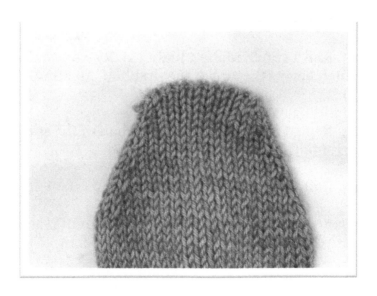

Someone with long, narrow feet may prefer the exact opposite to the wide wedge: a pointed toe. Rather than working the increases/decreases more frequently, there would be an additional knit round between the increase/decrease round, resulting in a long, tapered toe box. An example would be an increase/decrease round, then two knit rounds, and repeating that three-round pattern. This type of toe typically has fewer stitches to cinch or graft closed.

Toe-Up

Step 1: Using your choice of method, cast on the prescribed number of stitches and arrange needles so both halves of the sock are easily identified. Stitch markers are recommended but not necessary.

Step 2: Knit 1 round.

Step 3: Knit 1 stitch, Make 1 Right (M1R), knit to the last stitch before the end of the first half, Make 1 Left (M1L).

Step 4: Repeat Step 3 for the second half of the stitches in the round.

Step 5: Knit 2 rounds.

Step 6: Repeat Steps 3-5 until the stitch count reaches the desired circumference. Proceed to the foot.

Cuff-Down

Step 1: Ensure the stitches are arranged on the needles, so both halves are easily identified. After completing the foot of the sock, at the beginning of a round, knit 1 stitch, Slip Slip Knit (SSK) decrease, knit to the last 3 stitches, Knit 2 Together (K2TOG), knit the remaining stitch.

Step 2: Repeat Step 1 on the second half of the stitches.

Step 3: Knit 2 rounds.

Step 4: Repeat Steps 1-3 until about 6-8 stitches are remaining.

Step 5: Graft the toe closed using the desired method.

Tip #49: While England wasn't appreciative of Lee's invention, King Henri IV of France was more than willing to fund the venture. As a result, socks for the lower classes became more readily available.

Spiral Toe Instructions

One unexpected style of the toe is the spiral. The stitches are divided into an even number of sections with stitch markers, usually four, then increases/decreases are worked just before each marker on one round. The next round is knit normally, then the cycle repeats. The finished toe will appear pointier than a standard wedge, but many people swear by its comfort and look. Spiral toes work exceedingly well, being cinched as a finish instead of grafting.

Toe-Up

Step 1: Using your choice of method, cast on the prescribed number of stitches and divide them into four equal sections using stitch markers.

Step 2: Knit 1 round.

Step 3: Knit to the first Marker (M), Make 1 Right, slip Marker.

Step 4: Repeat Step 3 for the remaining Markers.

Step 6: Knit 1 round.

Step 6: Repeat Steps 3-5 until the stitch count reaches the desired circumference. Proceed to the foot.

Cuff-Down

Step 1: After completing the sock's foot, knit 1 round and place Markers to divide the toe into four equal sections.

Step 2: Knit to 2 stitches before the Marker, K2TOG.

Step 3: Repeat Step 2 for the remaining Markers.

Step 4: Knit 1 round.

Step 5: Repeat Steps 2-4 until 6-8 stitches remain.

Step 5: Cinch the toe closed by threading the tail through the remaining stitches and pulling tight.

Tip #50: Sock lengths changed drastically over the centuries. Depending on the fashion of the era, socks could come up as high as the mid-thigh or as low as the mid-calf.

Anatomically Correct Toe Instructions

The often-overlooked benefit of hand-knitting socks for a specific person is matching the socks to their feet, which includes the toes. Anatomically correct socks are possible, where the knitter adjusts, so that left and right socks have decreases on the appropriate sides (smaller toes) to create a slant leading up to the larger toes. A recipient who may not like socks feeling tight around the toes would benefit from anatomically correct socks as the gentle sloping will have less resistance than a wedge toe box as it is pulled onto the foot.

Toe-Up

Step 1: Using your choice of method, cast on the prescribed number of stitches and arrange them so that the left and right sides are easily identifiable. It is less necessary with the Toe-Up method if the knitter keeps track of where to put the heel in relation to the specific toe shape.

Step 2: Knit 1 round.

Step 3 (Left): Knit 1 stitch, M1R, knit to the last stitch in the round, M1L.

Step 3 (Right): Knit to 1 stitch before the end of the first half of stitches, M1L, knit 2, M1R, knit to the end of round.

Step 4: Knit 1 round.

Step 5: Repeat Steps 3-4 until the stitch count reaches the desired circumference.

Cuff-Down

Step 1: Arrange stitches so that the left and right sides of the sock are easily identifiable. Stitch markers are recommended but not necessary.

Step 3 (Left): Knit 1 stitch, SSK, knit to last 3 stitches in the round, K2TOG, knit 1.

Step 3 (Right): Knit to 3 stitches before the end of the first half of stitches, K2TOG, knit 2, SSK, knit to the end of round.

Step 4: Knit 1 round.

Step 5: Repeat Steps 3-4 until 10-12 stitches remain.

Step 6: Graft remaining stitches closed.

Rounded Toe Instructions

Perhaps the wearer of the sock prefers rounded edges over sharp ones, and in this case, a rounded toe is an excellent option. In a rounded toe, the sock's stitches are divided into many different sections with stitch markers; increases/decreases are worked just before each marker, then two rounds are knit. This pattern repeats until the desired stitch count, or there is only one stitch left in each section, and these remaining stitches are cinched closed.

Toe-Up

Step 1: Divide the stitches into 6-8 sections, depending on the stitch count and how long the toe needs to be; 6 sections will make a longer toe than 8 sections.

Step 2: Knit to 2 stitches before the marker, or end of a section, Knit the Front and Back of the stitch (KFB). Repeat to the end of the round.

Step 3: Knit 1 round.

Step 4: Repeat Steps 2-3 until half the desired number of stitches is reached.

Step 5: Knit to 2 stitches before the marker, or end of a section, KFB. Repeat to the end of the round.

Step 6: Knit 2 rounds.

Step 7: Repeat Steps 5-6 until the desired total number of stitches is reached.

Cuff-Down

Step 1: Divide the stitches into 6-8 sections, depending on the stitch count and how long the toe needs to be; 6 sections will make a longer toe than 8 sections.

Step 2: Knit to 2 stitches before the marker, or end of a section, K2TOG. Repeat to the end of the round.

Step 3: Knit 2 rounds.

Step 4: Repeat Steps 2-3 until half the number of original cast-on stitches remain.

Step 5: Knit to 2 stitches before the marker, or end of a section, K2TOG. Repeat to the end of the round.

Step 6: Knit 1 round.

Step 7: Repeat Steps 5-6 until 8 stitches remain.

Step 8: Cut the yarn, thread it through the remaining stitches, cinch to close, and weave in the ends.

Tip #52: The 1600s were also when decorations began to migrate from the tops of socks to be distributed throughout the entire sock.

Cinch or Graft?

When knitting from the cuff-down, which is preferable: grafting the toe or cinching it? Previous chapters have discussed methods of grafting to ensure a seamless toe. Cinching is when the knitter cuts the working yarn, threads it through the remaining stitches, and pulls tight to close the opening. Grafting is typically used with toe shapes that have decreases on opposite sides, such as a wedge because it is a linear finish. Cinching can be used with toe shapes where the decreases are knit in a spiral and compliment the circular finish to the sock.

Tip #53: Cotton made its way into public consumption for garments, including socks, in the late 1600s.

The Kitchener Stitch is the graft most widely known to the knitting community and is covered more in-depth later in Chapter 11. Cinching has fewer steps, is simpler to learn, and much quicker if the knitter is in a hurry.

Chapter Review

- A short, wide wedge would have increases/decreases more frequently on both sides of the sock
- A pointed toe would have increases/decreases less regularly on both sides of the sock
- A spiral toe would be divided into even sections for increases/decreases
- Anatomically correct toes will have more increases/decreases on the left or right side depending on which foot the sock will be worn
- A rounded toe can be increased/decreased in the same way a hat is worked
- Cinching a toe closed is suitable for rounded or spiral toes
- Grafting a toe closed is good for wide or straight toes

Chapter 7: Knitting the Foot of Your Sock

Top vs. Sole

In nearly all designs for socks that include a stitch pattern, the pattern is continued on the top of the foot, but not necessarily the sole. The reasons not to have the design on the sole can range from the fact that it will not be seen while the sock is worn to the fabric's strength in a pattern. Lace is more delicate than stockinette, making it more prone to breakage or additional holes (lace itself is already made up of strategically placed holes); it is not ideal for the sole of a sock.

Tip #62: Socks can absorb nearly one liter of sweat per day. The salinity can hasten the breakdown of feeble socks.

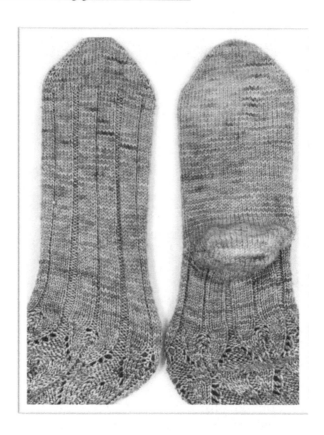

Ribbing can also be used on the sole if the wearer prefers a tighter sock in the foot. The same is also true for colorwork patterns. The additional strands of yarn used in colorwork add further strength to the fabric when carrying the unused "floats" along behind the work. Maintaining the intricate colorwork pattern is also more easily done when continued throughout the whole foot; it also allows the knitter's gauge to be more consistent.

Tip #54: Albert Einstein complained of holes wearing too quickly in his socks because of his large toes. Perhaps a hand-knit pair with a reinforced toe would have fared better!

Stitch markers or needle arrangements will assist the knitter in keeping track of which side of the sock is the sole and which is the top. Stitch markers can be placed at the beginning and end of the sock's top, or the stitches can be evenly distributed between circular needles or DPNs. It is usually more challenging to distinguish between the top of the sock and the sole when working from the toe-up, as using the cuff-down method would enable the knitter to utilize the heel to determine which side is the sole.

Tip #55: Early forms of knitting were called "nalbinding" or "sprang" and used to make fishing nets.

Determining Proper Length

Knitting socks from the toe-up requires several adjustments than what is more commonly done in the cuff-down method. How a knitter determines the length of the foot can change depending on the situation or pattern selected. Much of the time, a knitter need only work the foot of the sock until they reach the center of the ankle bone, then begin to work the heel. Short-row heels and afterthought heels can easily follow this determination.

Tip #65: Nalbinding FOs (finished objects) have dated back to 6500 BC in Israel.

This method of measurement can be tricky to accomplish when knitting socks for another person. Sox Therapist on Ravelry.com, designer of the exceedingly popular short-row heel known as the Fish Lips Kiss Heel, suggests that recipients of socks provide the knitter with a tracing of their foot and include a mark at the location of the ankle bone.

Tip #56: By 1000 AD, Vikings were wearing socks from nalbinding.

The choice of a riverbed gusset, however, changes the method of measurement. A gauge swatch will be crucial in helping determine when to begin the gusset prior to the heel. Once a knitter knows how many rows per inch they have with their tension, examining the pattern for the number of rows in the gusset will explain how far back from the heel to begin. For instance, if a knitter's gauge is six rows per inch, and there are 24 rows in the riverbed gusset, then the heel should begin four inches from the heel.

Tip #57: Nalbinding utilized one needle to link together short lengths of yarn. Egyptians pioneered the two-needle method known today as knitting.

Chapter Review

- Lace is not as good an option for the sole of the sock
- Stockinette is a good choice; ribbing is an option as well
- Colorwork strands add strength to the fabric
- Cuff-down socks can stop working the foot after the pinky toe

- Toe-up socks can stop working the socks before or at the ankle bone, depending on the heel type
- Stitch markers and needle arrangement can help distinguish between top and sole

Chapter 8: Knitting the Heel of Your Sock

Flap and Gusset

A slip stitch heel flap and gusset are unarguably the most common type of knitted heel in socks. The ease at which a knitter can achieve a strong, nearly dual-layer fabric is unparalleled among other heel options. Typically, a heel flap is knit over the second half of the stitches for an equal number of rows to create a square. The heel is then "turned" by working decreases over short rows to create a pocket. Additional stitches are picked up along the sides of the heel flap to bring the work back into the round. From there, the gusset is knitted by decreasing stitches symmetrically on each side of the sock until the original cast-on number is reached.

Tip #58: Egyptian knitters became so fast that they had to devise new methods to spin yarn to keep up with the demand. Enter: the Spinning Wheel.

Step 1 *(Begin heel flap)*: Knit across the first half of the stitches on the needles (otherwise known as the top of the foot or instep). The second half of the stitches will be knit flat, worked back and forth instead of in the round.

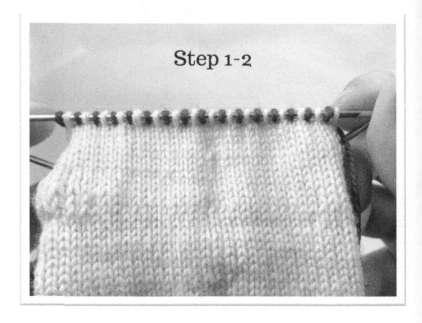

Step 2: Slip 1 stitch purl-wise with yarn in the back, knit the next stitch, and repeat these two stitches across the heel, ending with a knit stitch. Turn the work.

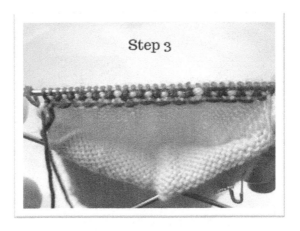

Step 3: Slip the first stitch purl-wise with yarn in the front this time, then purl the remaining stitches on the heel. Turn the work again.

Step 4: Repeat Steps 2 and 3 until the number of rows worked is the same as the number of stitches in the second half of the sock, ending after a purl row. (Example: 32 stitches across the heel, 32 rows worked total in the heel flap)

Step 5 *(Begin heel turn)*: Knit to one stitch past the heel center, slip the next two stitches onto the right needle knit-wise, and then knit them together through the back loops (Slip Slip Knit – SSK). Knit one more stitch, then turn the work without wrapping.

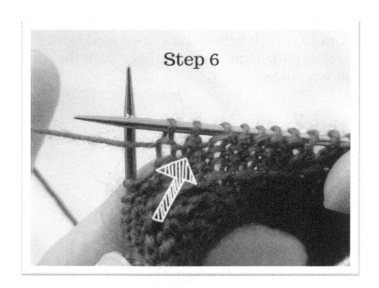

Step 6

Step 6: Slip the first stitch purl-wise with the yarn in front, purl 5-7 stitches (depending on heel width preference), then purl 2 together (P2TOG), and purl one more stitch. Turn the work without wrapping.

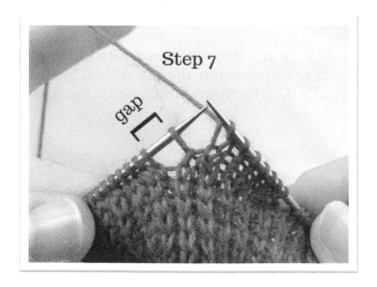

Step 7

gap

Step 7: Slip the first stitch purl-wise with the yarn in the back, knit to 1 stitch before the gap created by the decrease, SSK then knit 1 more stitch. Turn the work without wrapping.

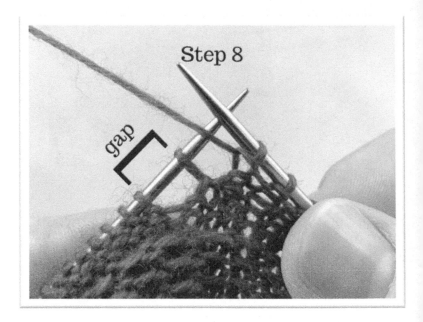

Step 8: Slip the first stitch purl-wise with the yarn in front, purl to 1 stitch before the gap created by the decrease, P2TOG, then purl 1 more stitch. Turn the work.

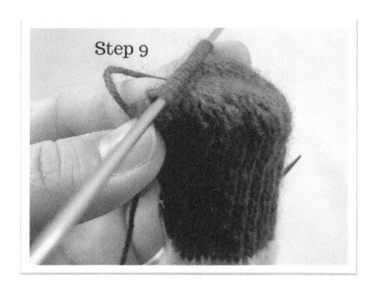

Step 9: Repeat Steps 7-8 until all heel stitches have been worked, ending with a single purl stitch. If the number of stitches does not finish on a purl, ending on the P2TOG is fine. Turn the work.

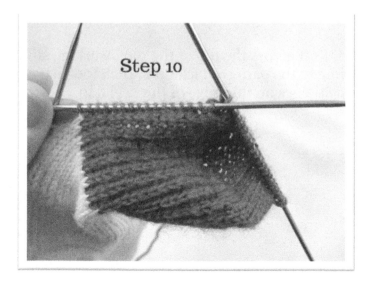

Step 10 *(Begin gusset)*: Knit across the heel stitches, then pick up 1 stitch for each of the slipped stitches on the edge. (Example: if 32 rows were worked, there would be 16 stitches to pick up)

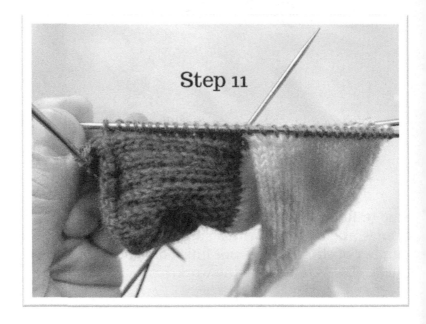

Step 11: Knit across the top of the foot, working stitches according to the pattern. Pick up 1 stitch for each of the slipped stitches on this edge of the heel flap.

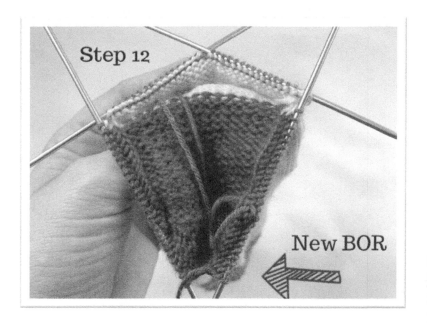

Step 12: Knit half of the remaining original heel stitches and place a stitch marker, which will be the new beginning of the round. Arrange the stitches on the needles, or place stitch markers, so that heel stitches are separate from the instep stitches on the top of the foot.

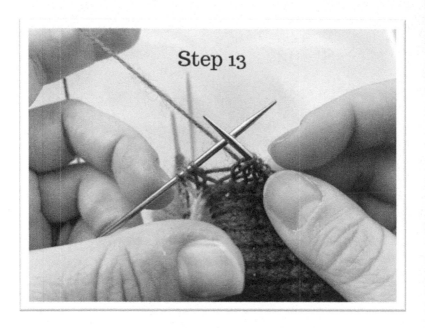

Step 13: From the new beginning of the round (BOR) marker, knit across to 3 stitches before the next needle or marker. K2TOG then knit the remaining stitch.

Step 14: Knit across the top of the foot, working stitches according to the pattern. Adjust the next needle or marker, then knit 1 stitch, SSK, and knit to the BOR marker.

Step 15: Knit one round.

Step 16: Repeat Steps 13-15 until the stitch count reaches the original cast-on number.

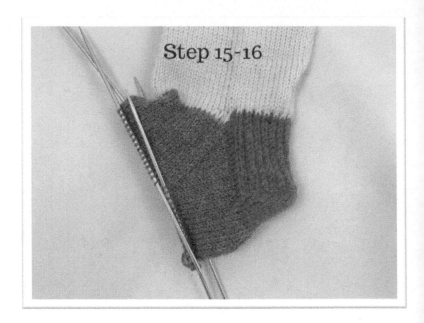

Step 15-16

The heel flap and gusset are complete!

Tip #69: In 1200 AD, European knitters started the circular knitting trend for tubes using five needles. This method leaves minimal seaming and can be done even quicker!

Short-Row Heel

As mentioned in previous chapters, a short-row heel is more easily worked into a toe-up sock than the flap and gusset heel. By working back and forth, first in shorter and shorter rows, then in longer and longer rows, the knitter can create a deeper pocket for the heel than is created with a heel turn. Many recipients enjoy the snug feeling of the negative ease provided by a short-row heel and prefer it over the flap and gusset.

Tip #59: Traders traversing the Indian Ocean introduced knitting to Iran and Iraq during the 1200s.

Step 1: Knit in pattern across the first half of the stitches, the ones on top of the foot, to the second half of stitches at the back. Knit to 2 stitches before the end of the heel stitches. Bring the yarn forward, slip the next stitch, wrap the thread around the slipped stitch, put the wrapped stitch back on the left needle, and turn the work. You have just completed a Wrap and Turn.

Step 2: Purl across the heel to 2 stitches before the end. Wrap and Turn.

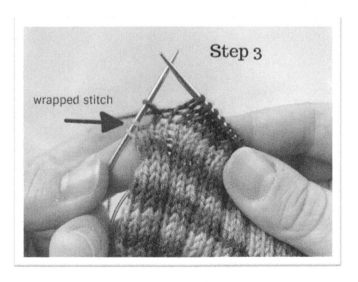

Step 3: Knit to 1 stitch before the last wrap, Wrap and Turn.

Step 4: Purl to 1 stitch before the wrap, Wrap and Turn.

Step 5: Repeat Steps 3-4 until about one-third of the heel stitches remain unwrapped in the center, ending after a purl Wrap and Turn.

Step 6: Knit across the heel, pick up wraps (optional) and knit them together with the stitches until the last stitch. Wrap and Turn.

Step 7: Purl across the heel, picking up the other wraps (optional) and purling them together with the stitches until the last stitch. Wrap and Turn.

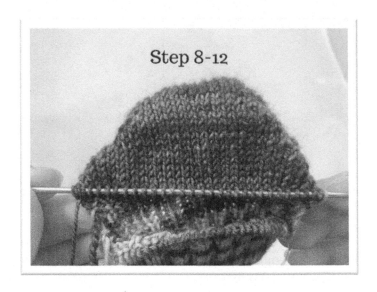

Step 8: Knit across two-thirds of the stitches on the heel, so you are just past the previously unwrapped center stitches. Wrap and Turn.

Step 9: Purl across the unwrapped center stitches. Wrap and Turn.

Step 10: Knit across to the wrapped stitch, pick up the wrap and knit it together with the stitch. Wrap and Turn the next stitch.

Step 11: Purl across to the wrapped stitch, pick up the wrap and purl it together with the stitch. Wrap and Turn the next stitch.

Step 12: Repeat Steps 10-11 until all the stitches have been worked, ending in a purl. Wrap and Turn on the very last stitch.

Step 13: Knit across the heel, work the instep in pattern as before, at the wrapped stitch at the beginning of the heel, pick up the wrap and knit it together with the stitch, knit across the heel once more.

The Short-Row Heel is complete!

Tip #60: While Egyptian knitters learned the purl stitch fairly early on, Europeans didn't seem to discover it until the 1500s!

Afterthought Heel

Aptly named, the Afterthought Heel can be worked once the rest of the sock has been completed. It is often used to keep from interrupting a striping or colorwork pattern or simply because a knitter wishes to put it off until the end. Typically, an Afterthought Heel is worked the same as a wedge toe, only beginning with more stitches. The knitter will take a piece of scrap yarn and knit across the heel stitches with that instead of the working yarn. After the heel is ready to be worked, the scrap yarn is removed, and two rows of live stitches are exposed and worked in the round.

Setup (while knitting the sock): Knit across the top of the foot in pattern, with a piece of scrap knit across the heel stitches. Slip the scrap yarn stitches back onto the left needle, then knit them with the working yarn. Complete the rest of the sock per pattern.

Step 1: Remove the scrap yarn and pick up both sets of now-live stitches. Arrange on either DPNs or circular needles (long enough for Magic Loop).

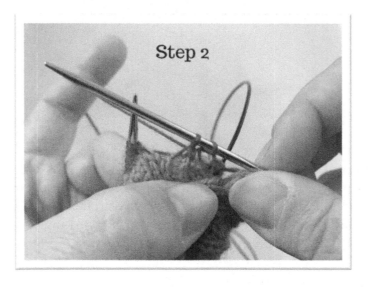

Step 2: Knit 1 stitch, SSK, then knit to the last 3 stitches on this side of the heel, K2TOG, and knit the final stitch. Repeat for the second side of the heel.

Step 3: Knit one round.

Step 4: Repeat Steps 2-3 until 6-8 stitches are remain (depending on heel width preference).

Step 5: Graft the heel closed with the Kitchener Stitch.

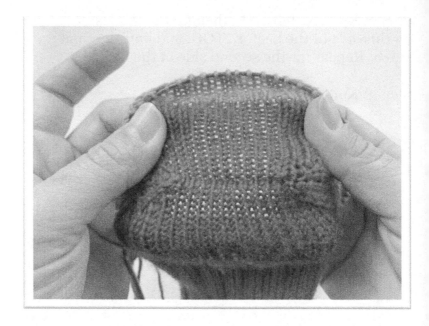

The Afterthought Heel is complete!

Tip #61: Knitting was not documented in China until the 1920s. After the White Russians suffered defeat in their civil war, they traveled to Eastern China and taught their caravan companions to knit.

Chapter Review

- Heels are typically knit over the second half of the stitches that were cast-on at the beginning
- Short-Row and Afterthought Heels can be worked either toe-up or cuff-down

- Flap and Gusset heels are more easily worked cuff-down but can be knit toe-up with some modifications
- A Gusset contains stitches that are picked up and gradually decreased over several rounds
- The Short-Row Heel is knit back and forth while the Afterthought Heel is worked in the round

Chapter 9: Knitting the Leg of Your Sock

For some knitters, the sock's leg is the most painful part to work because it can feel like a long slog. It is especially true if the sock is being knit in the Stockinette stitch, hundreds of knit stitches on a seemingly endless loop. Knitters in all centuries managed to find ways to liven up working through the legs of socks, from stripes to colorwork and cables to ribbing. As the most likely section of sock to be seen, the opportunity for creativity can be irresistible for many crafters.

Tip #62: The men from China in the caravan with the White Russians would spin yarn from their camels' hair as they traveled. Knitting socks and extra garments to sell became common practice.

Determining Length

Historically speaking, a wide range of lengths for socks has come in and out of fashion. From short socks with split toes for sandals to long socks that are tied above the knee with garters, no portion of the leg has been left untouched by socks at some point in time. It can be daunting for some knitters to tackle a potentially large project with such a wide array to choose from.

Tip #63: During World War II, wool was not widely available due to shortages; Brits were encouraged to rip out old or unwearable knitwear to re-use the yarn.

Ankle Length or No-Show Socks

Socks that fall just below or just above the ankle bone can be excellent for the beginning sock knitter. The short length makes for a faster project and less time between cast-on and wearing the final product, something many beginners (and even advanced knitters) appreciate immensely. One benefit to short socks is not having to worry as much about whether the entire sock will fit over the heel and instep, which is the thickest part of the foot. It can be challenging to have the correct balance of ease and gauge for the heel and instep in a method such as colorwork as it has much less elasticity than other methods.

Ankle socks may or may not need a ribbed cuff, depending on the final length and wearer's preferences. A below-the-ankle sock does just as well with a rolled edge, achieved by simply binding off after an inch or two of Stockinette stitch, as with a ribbed cuff. One excellent example of an ankle sock with a rolled cuff is the Rose City Rollers pattern by Mara Catherine Bryner (Ravelry.com Username: Maracatherine). This free pattern goes cuff-down (though it is easily adapted for toe-up) by knitting a few rounds in Stockinette before jumping right into the heel flap and gusset. For beginners or knitters who dislike working through a sock's leg, this pattern is excellent for near-instant gratification on a project.

Tip #76: Another good ankle sock pattern for beginners is "Easy Peasy Socks for First-Timers" by Stacey Trock, and it's also available On Ravelry.com

Crew Length Socks

The length of crew socks comes to most peoples' minds when they think about knitting socks, and, as a result, most available patterns are written for it. Crew socks rise above the ankle and stop just before the calf begins. A good approach to remember, if trying on the socks as they are knitted is not preferable for any reason, is the leg and cuff can match the length of the foot and toe. If working toe-up, fold the sock in half to check the length and remember to leave room for the cuff. For cuff-down socks, the leg can be compared to the length of the recipient's actual foot or a tracing if done.

Crew socks have just enough length for beautiful patterns of colorwork, stripes, cables, ribbing, or other textures, but not so much length that a knitter requires more than one skein of sock yarn (about 400 yards). Even large men's crew socks can usually be knitted in 400 yards or less, depending on the knitter's gauge.

Tip #64: An excellent example of a crew sock pattern would be the Rye socks mentioned in Tip #33 by TinCanKnits!

Adjusting Width

As socks migrate farther and farther up the wearer's leg, chances are higher that the width of the socks will need to be adjusted. Once socks begin to get into Over-The-Knee and Thigh Length territory, the width almost certainly will need to be increased. Not many people have the same width at their ankles as they do at their thighs. A good, solid ribbed cuff is exceedingly helpful in ensuring the socks stay put at the height they are meant for; some knitters have also included eyelets to thread an I-Cord or lace through to tie the socks around the leg.

Tip #65: I-Cord is a length of knitted cord, usually composed of 3 stitches knit in the same order on a pair of DPNs. A quick recipe for I-Cord can be found in the Appendix.

Knee Length Socks

Knee-High socks come up over the calf and fall just below the knee. While similar to Boot Length, Knee High socks are a bit longer. The sock's cuff and leg will both need to be loose enough to accommodate the calf muscle but tight enough to keep from falling down the leg. Negative ease can provide an advantage in this area, especially if provided by ribbing or lace.

Over-The-Knee socks do what their name says: come up over the knee but stop short of the thigh. Though many knitters do work Over-The-Knee socks in fingering weight yarn, this is a fantastic introduction to Worsted weight socks for beginning sock knitters. The heavier weight creates larger stitches, making the inches fly by while knitting through them, even in lace or ribbing.

Tip #66: Very Tall Socks by Kelly Griffith is a simple Aran weight pattern (even heavier than Worsted!) that can be worked as long or as short as desired. It can be found on Ravelry.com via this URL: www.ravelry.com/patterns/library/very-tall-socks.

Thigh High Socks

Perhaps the second oldest of sock heights, the Thigh High has a long, rich history through numerous cultures and eras. From Medieval Europe to modern citizens worldwide, Thigh High socks have been providing warmth and protection all the way up wearers' legs for centuries. Originally worn with garters made up of ribbon or lace before evolving to belts and clips in the early 20th Century, Thigh High socks have always struggled to find that delicate balance between what will fit the whole leg while also staying in place.

An intriguing example of a creative knitter solving the centuries-old problem has been lace-up socks. By creating an area through which to thread either lace or I-Cord, the wearer can cinch up the socks exactly as tight or as loose as necessary throughout the length of their leg. Depending on the bulk of the socks, these may or may not be appropriate for wear with shoes, but as slippers around the house, they will certainly always be lovely. There is a free pattern available on Ravelry.com for lace-up Thigh High socks called Nyörisukat by Eini Kivelä available through this URL: www.ravelry.com/patterns/library/nyorisukat.

Tip #67: Knitting was still widely taught as a useful skill up through the 1950s and 1960s in Europe and the United States but saw a sharp decline in the 1980s due to the rise in popularity of tracksuits and sweatshirts.

Chapter Review

- Ankle socks are suitable for beginners due to their quick finish
- Crew Length socks have the most patterns written for their length
- Knee Length socks can fall just under or just over the knee and do well with a well-knit ribbed cuff
- Thigh High socks may need additional support to stay up, such as garters or laces

Chapter 10: Knitting the Cuff of Your Sock

Ribbed Cuff

Ribbed cuffs are the most used for hand-knitted socks--and with good reason! Not only are they a classic look that never goes out of style, but the negative ease provides a natural elasticity in its construction. Negative ease is a way of describing a tighter fitting fabric that can stretch to meet its wearer's needs.

Tip #68: In the 1990s, knitting was approached with renewed interest primarily due to the accessibility of the internet. As the internet grew, so did the knitting community.

Toe-Up

Step 1: Change the color of yarn, if appropriate, and knit 1 round in new color.

Step 2: Begin ribbing pattern; K1P1 or K2P2 are common rib stitch combinations.

Step 3: Repeat Step 2 until the cuff measures desired length, typically 2-3 inches.

Step 4: Bind off.

Cuff-Down

Step 1: Cast-on the desired number of stitches using the preferred cast-on method.

Step 2: Begin ribbing pattern; K1P1 or K2P2 are common rib stitch combinations.

Step 3: Repeat Step 2 until the cuff measures desired length, typically 2-3 inches.

Step 4: Change the color of yarn now if applicable.

Tip #69: The first online magazine for knitters, KnitNet, began publishing in 1998.

Garter Stitch Cuff

Garter Stitch tends to be overlooked by knitters as it is usually the first type of stitch they learn before moving on to more complicated patterns. As a cuff for a sock, it is a delightful change of pace from the vertical lines provided by ribbing in most other socks. Horizontal ridges, squishy bumps on both sides, what is not to love about a surprisingly efficient cuff?

Toe-Up

Step 1: Knit 1 round even.

Step 2: Purl 1 round.

Step 3: Repeat Steps 1-2 until the cuff measures the desired length and bind off loosely.

Cuff-Down

Step 1: Cast-on the desired number of stitches using the preferred Cast-On method.

Step 2: Knit 1 round even.

Step 3: Purl 1 round.

Step 4: Repeat Steps 2-3 until the cuff measures the desired length and change yarn if applicable.

Lace Cuff

Lace cuffs can make for a bold statement or a delicate finishing touch. Lace can provide positive ease that allows it extra stretchy capacity, an excellent feature if the cuff rests on the wearer's calves or thighs. Positive ease is a way of describing a looser fabric that has "extra space."

Toe-Up

Step 1: If working with an even number of stitches, knit the first stitch of the round. Next, work a Yarn Over (YO), then a K2tog, and repeat these two stitches until one stitch before the end of the round. Knit the last stitch. If working with an odd number of stitches, omit the last knit stitch.

Step 2: Knit 1 round.

Step 3: Repeat Steps 1-2 until the cuff measures desired length.

Step 4: Bind off (BO) loosely or with a stretchy BO.

Cuff-Down

Step 1: Cast-on the desired number of stitches with the preferred method.

Step 2: If working with an even number of stitches, knit the first stitch of the round. Next, work a Yarn Over (YO), then a K2tog, and repeat these two stitches until one stitch before the end of the round. Knit the last stitch. If working with an odd number of stitches, omit the last knit stitch.

Step 2: Knit 1 round.

Step 4: Repeat Steps 2-3 until the cuff measures desired length.

Step 5: Continue to the leg of the sock.

Chapter Review

- Ribbed cuffs are most used and provide natural elasticity
- Garter cuffs create eye-catching horizontal lines
- Lace cuffs are excellent for wider sections of the leg, such as calves or thighs

Chapter 11: Binding Off and Finishing Your Knitted Socks

Knitted Bind Off (Toe-Up)

The Knitted Bind Off is commonly the first bind off a new knitter learns because of how similar it is to the knit stitch. However, the name is a bit of a misnomer as it could also be called the Purled Bind Off or Ribbed Bind Off. The knitter has the choice of either purling or knitting, or both while working the bind off.

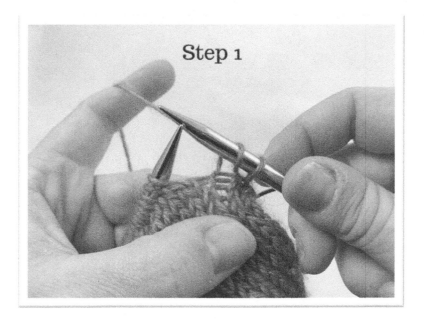

Step 1: Knit 2 stitches.

Step 2: Pass the first stitch over the second stitch and off the needle. The first stitch has been bound off.

Step 3: Knit 1 stitch.

Step 4: Repeat Steps 2-3 until there is 1 stitch remaining.

Step 5: Knit the remaining stitch, then cut the yarn and pull it through the last stitch to tighten.

JSSBO: Jeny's Surprisingly Stretchy Bind off (Toe-Up)

In the fall of 2009, Knitty.com published a new bind-off designed by Jeny Staiman, and the world of sock knitters rejoiced! Abbreviated as JSSBO, Jeny's Surprisingly Stretchy Bind Off became the go-to bind-off for many a sock knitter. It is more elastic than the sewn bind-off methods Nanas and Grans were taught as they were coming up.

Knit Stitch Instructions:

Step 1: Knit 1, reverse Yarn Over, Knit 1.

Step 2: Insert the needle into both the YO and the first knit stitch, pass both over the second knit stitch.

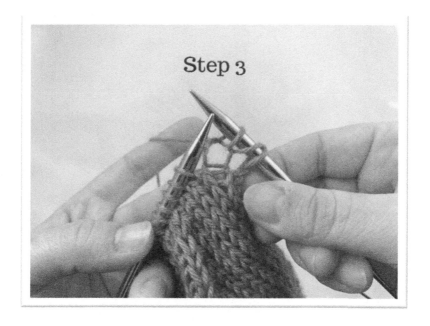

Step 3: Reverse YO, knit 1.

Step 4: Repeat Steps 2-3 until 1 stitch remains.

Step 5: Cut the yarn and pull it through the last stitch to tighten.

<u>Purl Stitch Instructions:</u>

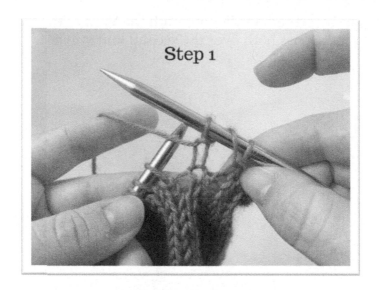

Step 1: Purl 1, YO (in the normal direction), Purl 1.

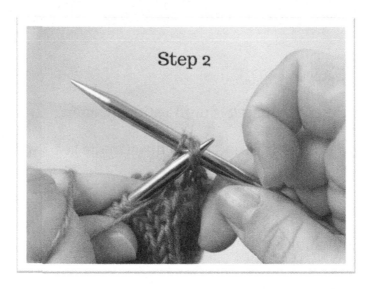

Step 2: Insert the needle into both the YO and the first purl stitch, pass both over the second purl stitch.

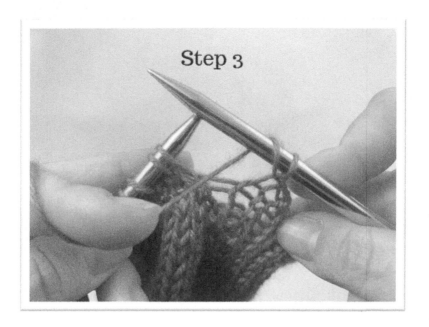

Step 3: YO, purl 1.

Step 4: Repeat Steps 2-3 until 1 stitch remains.

Step 5: Cut the yarn and pull it through the last stitch to tighten.

If the knitter is utilizing JSSBO with a ribbed cuff, the instructions can be worked in tandem. The reverse YO will be done before a knit stitch, and the regular YO will be worked before the purl stitch. Passing both over remains the same.

Kitchener Stitch (Cuff-Down)

Both an eternal favorite and the bane of knitter's existence, the Kitchener Stitch has a highly polarized fan base. An example of a sewn bind-off, the Kitchener Stitch, requires a tapestry needle and knitting needles. For the toes of socks, this sewn bind-off is relatively quick and painless; however, the difficulty increases in parallel with the number of stitches. It can be challenging to keep track of which step the knitter was on if suddenly distracted and looking back to their work.

Setup: Arrange the stitches in even rows, one on each needle, with the tips of the needles pointing to the right. Cut the working yarn, leaving a long enough tail for the BO, and insert the end through a tapestry needle.

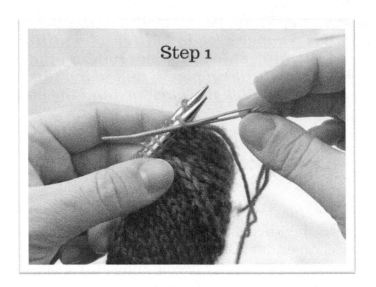

Step 1: Thread the tapestry needle through the front stitch purl-wise, leaving it on the knitting needle, pull the yarn all the way through, being careful not to ensnare the knitting needles.

Step 2: Thread the tapestry needle through the backstitch knit-wise, leaving it on the knitting needle, pulling the yarn through.

Step 3: Thread the tapestry needle through the front stitch knit-wise, slipping the front stitch off the knitting needle.

Step 4: Thread the tapestry needle through the next front stitch purl-wise, leaving the stitch on the knitting needle.

Step 5: Thread the tapestry needle through the backstitch purl-wise, slipping the stitch off the knitting needle.

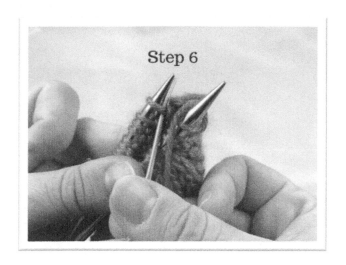

Step 6: Thread the tapestry needle through the next back stitch knit-wise, leaving the stitch on the knitting needle.

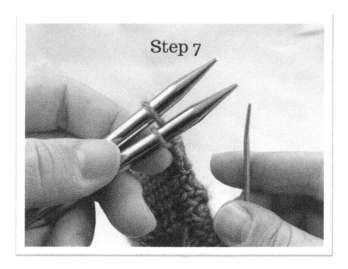

Step 7: Repeat Steps 5-8 until all stitches are bound off except two, one on each knitting needle.

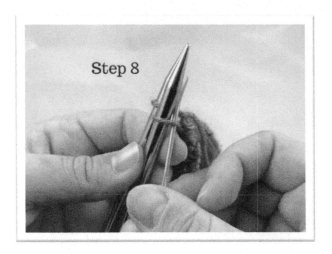

Step 8: Thread the tapestry needle through the front stitch knit-wise, slipping the front stitch off the knitting needle.

Step 9: Thread the tapestry needle through the backstitch purl-wise, slipping the stitch off the knitting needle.

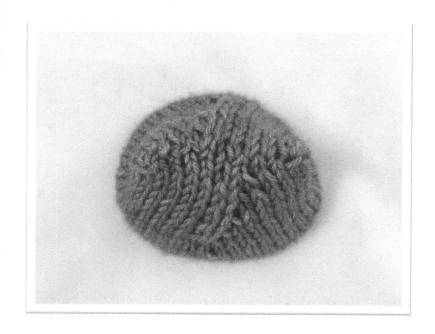

Three Needle Bind Off (Cuff-Down)

This bind-off is worked almost as a graft; however, it is still considered a knitted bind-off. The Three Needle Bind Off requires an additional needle, ideally smaller in size as the needles used on the sock, equal or one size up, will do in a pinch. Whether the extra needle is a DPN, a straight needle, or one of a pair of circular needles, this bind-off will still be achievable.

Step 1: Evenly distribute the remaining stitches onto two needles and hold them parallel.

Step 2: Insert the third needle knit-wise into the first stitch on the front needle, then knit-wise into the first stitch back needle.

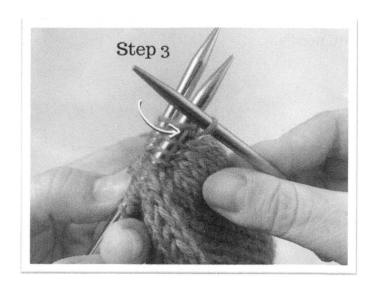

Step 3: Wrap the yarn around the third needle as if to knit, pull the needle through both stitches and allow both to fall off their respective needles.

Step 4: Repeat Steps 2-3. There are now two stitches on the third needle.

Step 5: Lift the first stitch on the third needle over the second stitch, as if doing a Knitted Bind Off.

Step 6: Repeat Steps 2-3 and 5 until all stitches but one are bound off.

Step 7: Pull the yarn through the last stitch.

Weaving in Ends

Just as there are many ways to knit socks, there are many ways to weave (or sew) in the ends of yarn once the socks are complete. Newer knitters may ask why they should weave in the ends at all; why wouldn't a knot suffice? The answer is that knots can come undone and drop stitches without notice. The safest, most secure way to ensure the ends stay put is to weave them into the back of the fabric. Ideally, what will happen is that the friction from the foot will cause the yarn to slightly felt to itself on the inside of the sock, fastening those ends into place completely.

Tip #77: Katherine Hepburn used to knit between takes on the sets of her films.

Felting is a process where when the yarn is combined with friction and heat, the scales on the individual staples (hairs) will start to rise and lock together even across stitches. Completed felted projects have no discernable single stitches and look like a solid piece of fabric. Slightly felted insides of socks still have stitch definition; however, the ends are more firmly rooted in their places.

It is also recommended that tails that have been woven in or secured not be cut until after blocking have been completed. Blocking or soaking the project in tepid water, then shaping or stretching it to dry, allows the yarn to relax. The yarn stores kinetic energy in its twists from being spun; the blocking process allows that energy to disperse and not hold as tight. Ends that are snipped too closely before blocking could potentially come loose after blocking, then be challenging to secure again.

Tip #78: Tom Hanks pranked Julia Roberts on the set of their movie Larry Crowne by giving the crew needles and yarn to surprise her.

Weave as You Go

Many knitters opt to weave their tails in as they work through the project. It is incredibly efficient when working with stripes, and there are multiple ends of multiple colors. Addressing the ends before finishing the socks is an excellent way to avoid a headache later. Doing the ends sooner rather than later means there is one less thing in the way of wearing the finished socks.

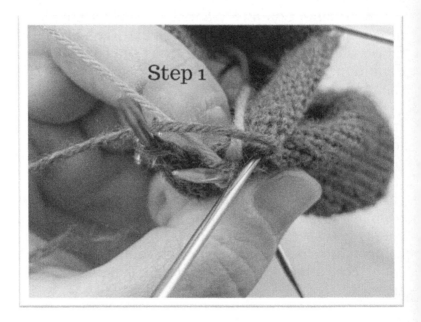

Step 1: Work the first 2-3 stitches in the new color, new round, or new row with the working yarn.

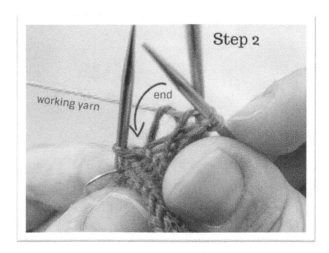

Step 2: On the wrong side of the fabric (inside the sock), lay the tail to be woven in across the top of the working yarn right to left.

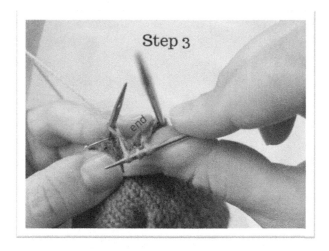

Step 3: Work the next stitch in pattern, but do not catch the tail. Allow the working yarn and new stitch to hold it in place on the back of the work.

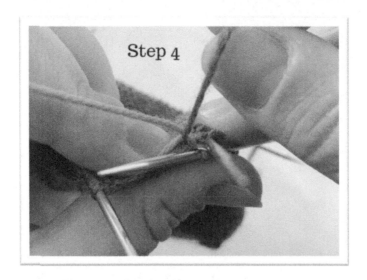

Step 4: Lay the tail across the top of the working yarn, this time left to right.

Step 5: Repeat Steps 2-4 until the tail has been woven behind 8-10 stitches.

Step 6: **Optional** - If planning to block socks, do not cut the tail's remaining length until after blocking to allow for any additional ease provided by the yarn relaxing.

__Tip #79: The World's Longest Knitted Scarf was knitted by Helge Johansen in Oslo, Norway. The scarf measures 14,978ft and 6.16in. Suddenly a pair of socks doesn't seem too difficult.__

Medium/Long Ends

When patterns mention how long of a tail to leave, this is generally an estimation erring on the side of caution. Two inches? Six inches? Most of the time, if the tail is only going to be sewn in later, eyeballing 3-4 inches is perfectly acceptable. If the tail needs to be used to graft something closed, such as a toe or heel, substantially more yarn is necessary. Once a knitter has finished a few projects, they have an idea of how much tail to leave themselves to weave in at the end.

Step 1: Thread the end through the eye of a tapestry needle.

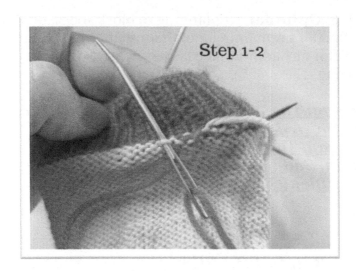

Step 2: On the wrong side of the fabric, inside the sock, weave the tapestry needle through the back of the stitches in one direction.

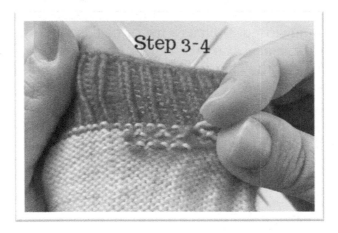

Step 3: Weave the tapestry needle through the back of the stitches in the opposite direction. Ensure the woven tail is not visible from the outside of the sock.

Step 4: Repeat Steps 2-3 as necessary, then cut or trim the tail's remaining length. If blocking the socks, do not trim the tail until after blocking.

Tip #80: Elizabeth Bond created the World's Largest Needles in Wiltshire, UK. The needles measure 14ft 6.33in long with a diameter of 3.54in.

Short Ends

Short ends happen. Whether an end is snipped too early, blocking stretched the fabric out, or a Long Tail Cast-On turned out not to be so long, after all, there is always a way to address a short end. This method may take some practice, and there are special needles available with larger eyes, but it is possible with a standard tapestry needle and some creative angling.

Step 1: Weave the empty tapestry needle through the backs of stitches near the yarn's short end. The eye of the needle should land near the end to be woven in.

Step 2: Gently thread the short tail through the eye of the tapestry needle, keeping the point woven through the backs of stitches.

Step 3: Pull the tapestry needle through the stitches. The tail may not weave all the way through the selected stitches, but that is ok. The end is now secure.

Step 4: **Optional** – If blocking the socks, do not trim any excess off the short end until after blocking is complete.

Tip #81: The World's Largest Knitted Blanket was a collaboration between 1,000 knitters from 32 countries. It was assembled in Ennis, Ireland, and, once finished, measured 21,471.95 square feet. It was then divided into smaller blankets which the Irish Red Cross received as a massive donation.

Chapter Review

- Ends woven inside of socks can felt and lock into place
- Ideally, weaving ends should happen after blocking
- Weaving as you go is an efficient method when working with stripes
- Long or medium tails should be woven in for some length rather than knotted
- Short ends can be woven in; however, it is typically in only one direction

Appendix: Sock Recipes

This section includes the "recipes" of the various sock elements used to create the example socks pictured in the previous chapters. Both Toe-Up and Cuff-Down recipes are written here; the final numbers may differ between knitters due to gauge. Trying on the sock as its knit is a great way to ensure proper fit. Additionally, a recipe for I-Cord is included for adventurous knitters who may be interested in securing their socks by tying them around the leg.

Tip #82: The World's Longest Finger Knitting piece was made by Ida Sofie Myking Veseth in Lonevåg, Norway. It was 63,548ft and 2.7in long and took more than 7 hours to measure for the record.

I-Cord Recipe

Notions:
- < 100yds
- 2 DPNs

Steps:

1. Cast-on 3-4 sts using the Long Tail Cast-On.
2. Slide the stitches to the other end of the DPN; the working yarn should be coming from the last stitch.
3. Knit all the stitches.
4. Repeat Steps 2-3 until the I-Cord has reached the desired length.

5. Cinch the stitches closed and thread the tails down the center of the cord to weave in.

Tip #83: The Longest Scarf Knitted by a Team took 2000 knitters three years. The final length was an astounding 33.74 MILES. The scarf was then turned into smaller blankets and donated to charity.

Toe-Up Socks

Notions:
- US size 0 circular knitting needles
- 200-400yds Main Color (MC) of sock yarn

Optional:
- Stitch marker
- 200yds of Contrast Color (CC) of sock yarn

Steps:

Cast-On and Toe Increases
1. Using Judy's Magic Cast-On, cast-on (CO) 10 sts per needle of MC (**Optional**: CO in CC if going for a contrasting toe/heel/cuff look).
2. Place Marker (PM) if using one, then Knit (K) across the first needle.
3. Knit Through Back Loop (KTBL) across the second needle.
4. K1, Make 1 Right (M1R) by lifting the bar between the stitches from behind and knitting through the front loop.
5. K to the last stitch on the needle.

6. Make 1 Left (M1L) by lifting the bar between the stitches from the front and knitting through the back loop, then K the last st.
7. Repeat Steps 4-6 on the second needle. (4sts added this round)
8. K all the way around.
9. Repeat Steps 4-7 until there are 32sts per needle (64sts total).
10. **Optional**: Change to MC here if doing contrasting toe/heel/cuff.

Foot and Heel
11. K3, Purl (P) 1 all the way around.
12. Repeat Step 11 until the foot of the sock is 2 inches shorter than the desired length or until the sock reaches the middle of the ankle bone.
13. K across the first needle (top of the foot)
14. **Optional**: Change to CC here if doing contrasting toe/heel/cuff.
15. K to 2 sts from the end of the second needle (sole of the foot, about to become the heel).
16. Bring the working yarn forward as if to Purl, slip the next st purl-wise onto the right needle, and bring the working yarn to the back again. Turn the needles, so the wrong side (the inside) is facing you. It is called a Wrap and Turn (W&T).
17. P to the last two sts on the heel, W&T.
18. K to 1 st before the last wrapped stitch, W&T.
19. P to 1 st before the last wrapped stitch, W&T.
20. Repeat Steps 16-17 until there are 11 wrapped sts on each side.
21. K across the heel, picking up the wraps and knitting them with the stitches as you go, W&T the last st.
22. P across the heel, picking up the wraps and purling them with the stitches as you go, W&T the last st.
23. K21, W&T

24. P10, W&T
25. K to the wrapped stitch and knit it together with the wrap, W&T the next st.
26. P to the wrapped stitch and purl it together with the wrap, W&T the next st.
27. Repeat Steps 23-24 until the 2nd to last st is wrapped on each side (2 wrapped sts will be next to each other.
28. K across the heel.
29. **Optional**: Change back to MC here if doing contrasting toe/heel/cuff.
30. K3P1 across the top of the foot.
31. K across the heel.
32. Repeat Steps 27-28 for approximately 1 inch.

Leg and Cuff
33. K3P1 around until the leg of the sock reaches the desired length.
34. **Optional**: Change to CC here if doing contrasting toe/heel/cuff, and K one more round.
35. K1P1 around for 1-2 inches.
36. Use Jeny's Surprisingly Stretchy Bind Off and weave in the ends.

Repeat above the steps for the second sock.

Tip #84: The World's Fastest Knitter is Miriam Tegels, who set the record of 118 stitches in a minute at the Swalmen Townhall, Netherlands, in 2006.

Cuff-Down Socks

Notions:
- US size 0 circular or double-pointed knitting needles
- 200-400yds Main Color (MC) of sock yarn
- Stitch marker

Optional:
- 200yds of Contrast Color (CC) of sock yarn

Cast-On, Cuff, and Leg
1. Using the Knitted Cast-On, cast-on (CO) 64 of MC (**Optional**: CO in CC if going for a contrasting toe/heel/cuff look).
2. Evenly distribute the stitches among the needles, being careful not to twist. **Optional**: Place Marker (PM) at the beginning of the round.
3. Knit 1 (K1), Purl 1 (P1) for 1-2 inches.
4. **Optional**: Change to MC here if doing contrasting toe/heel/cuff.
5. K across all needles until the leg of the sock reaches the desired length.

Heel Flap and Heel Turn

6. K across the first half of the stitches (top of the foot).
7. **Optional**: Change to CC here if doing contrasting toe/heel/cuff.
8. (Slip 1 with the yarn in the back (S1 WYIB), K1) across the second half of the stitches. You should have alternating slipped stitches and knit stitches all the way across. This is the Right Side (RS) of the Heel Flap.

9. Turn the work, so the Wrong Side (WS) faces you, S1 then P across.
10. RS: (S1, K1) across. Turn.
11. WS: S1, (P) across. Turn.
12. Repeat Steps 10-11 until the Heel Flap is 32 rows long.
13. K18, slip the next two stitches onto the right needle knit-wise, then knit them together through the back loops (Slip Slip Knit – SSK), K1. Turn.
14. S1 with the yarn in front (WYIF), P5, Purl 2 together (P2TOG), P1 Turn.
15. S1 WYIB, K to 1 stitch before the gap, SSK, K1. Turn.
16. S1 WYIF, P to 1 stitch before the gap, P2TOG, P1. Turn.
17. Repeat Steps 15-16 until all stitches of the heel flap have been worked. There will be fewer stitches on your needles; this is ok!
18. (RS) K across.
19. **Optional**: Change to MC here if doing contrasting toe/heel/cuff.

Gusset, Foot, and Toe

20. Pick up 1 stitch for each of the slipped stitches on the edge of the heel flap (16).
21. K across the top of the foot.
22. Pick up 1 stitch for each of the slipped stitches on the other side of the heel flap (16).
23. K across half the heel flap stitches (not the stitches picked up in the last round) and Place Marker (PM); this is the new beginning of the round.
24. Arrange the stitches on the needles so that the heel flap and gusset are on the "back" of the sock

and the top of the foot/instep stitches are on the "front."

    a. DPN – Needles 1 and 2 would have the back, Needles 3 and 4 would have the front.

    b. Circular Needles – Needle 1 would have the back, Needle 2 would have the front.

25. From marker K to the last 3 sts in the gusset, K2TOG, K1.

26. K across the front of the sock.

27. At the beginning of the gusset, K1, SSK, K to the end of the round.

28. K across the entire round.

29. Repeat Steps 25-28 until 64 sts remain on the needles (the original CO number).

30. K across all needles until the sock is 2in away from the tip of the foot.

31. **Optional**: Change to CC here if doing contrasting toe/heel/cuff.

32. K1, SSK,

33. K across the top of the toe to the last three stitches, knit 2 stitches together (K2TOG), K1.

34. Repeat Steps 17-18 on the bottom of the toe. (4sts decreased total)

35. K one round.

36. For the top and bottom of the toe: K1, SSK, K to last 3 sts, K2TOG, K1.

37. K one round.

38. Repeat Steps 20-21 until 10-14 sts are remaining.

39. Using Kitchener Stitch, graft the toe closed, then weave in any ends.

Repeat above the steps for the second sock.

Tip #85: North America's Fastest Knitter (and the world's second-fastest) is Linda Benne of Toronto, Canada, who knit 353 stitches in three minutes.

Glossary

DPN – Double Pointed Needle, a method to knit "in the round"

Magic Loop/Traveling Loop – another technique to knit "in the round"

Judy's Magic Cast-On – a seamless cast-On for toe-up socks

Jeny's Surprisingly Stretchy Bind Off – a stretchy Bind Off for toe-up socks

Fish Lips Kiss Heel – a pattern for a short row heel by Sox Therapist, Ravelry.com

LYS – Local Yarn Shop

BFL – Bluefaced Leicester

FO – Finished Object

MC – Main Color

CC – Contrast Color

Tip #86: The Longest Thread of Hand-Spun Wool in one hour was 326ft and 27in by Ruth Gough of Huddersfield, UK in 2011.

Stitch Abbreviations:

CO – Cast-On

K – Knit

P - Purl

St(s) – Stitch(es)

KFB – Knit through the front and back legs of one stitch.

M1R – Make 1 Right by lifting the bar between the stitches from behind and knitting through the front loop.

M1L – Make 1 Left by lifting the bar between the stitches from the front and knitting through the back loop.
SSK – slip two stitches onto the right needle knit-wise and knit them together through the back loops.
K2TOG – Knit 2 together
P2TOG – Purl 2 together
KTBL – Knit Through Back Loop
W&T – Wrap and Turn

Tip #87: It's not knitted, but game recognizes game: the World's Largest Granny Square was completed in 2015 by Stephen Duneier of Santa Barbara, California. The square contained more than 500,000 double crochet stitches, measured 1,311 square feet, and weighed more than 60 pounds!

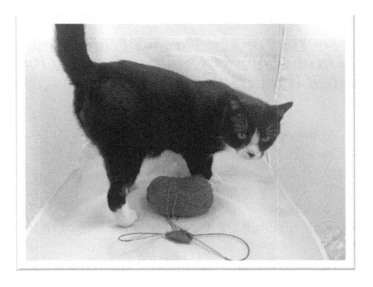

Frequently Asked Questions

General FAQs

Is it hard to knit socks?

Knitting socks requires the same level of skill as knitting a hat. If you can knit a hat, then you can undoubtedly knit socks! Basic sock patterns typically include the following types of stitches: knits, purls, slip stitches, SSKs (Slip Slip Knit – decrease), and K2TOGs (Knit 2 Together – decrease). Some patterns may contain W&Ts (Wrap & Turn – short rows), PSSOs (Pass Slipped Stitch Over – decrease), Kitchener stitches, or a type of seamless cast-on. If you get stuck on a specific stitch, YouTube has many helpful videos demonstrating just about everything. Overall, the trickiest part of knitting socks is the yarn's size, and if fingering weight yarn is too intimidating at first, feel free to start on worsted weight!

Is knitting easier to learn than crochet?

Knitting and crochet use one or multiple tools to turn loops and knots of yarn into stitches, which are turned into projects. This is where their similarities end. Knitted stitches, much like links in a chain, require the support of the stitches around them. Crocheted stitches have significantly less need for this level of support. As a result, crochet projects can provide less rigidity in terms of the overall structure; it's easier to branch off and work on one section then come back and do another. With crochet, you're dealing with only a few "live" stitches (they will come undone if you remove the hook) at a time.

In contrast, knitting is comprised almost entirely of live stitches. Crochet also takes up nearly twice as much yarn as knitting for an equivalent number of stitches. Whether knitting or crochet is "easier" to learn than the other is up to the individual, some people find one more complex than the other at first. If you can try both, then certainly try both! If not, then perhaps watch videos of knitting and crocheting for beginners and see what appeals to you. Finished projects are another item to consider. If there is one type of project, you like the look of; start with that!

How do I count stitches and rows?

Because we are knitting from right to left, we will also count stitches from right to left. Unless otherwise specified in a pattern, each loop on the needle is considered 1 stitch. If working through a whole lot of stitches, many knitters will utilize stitch markers placed at specific intervals to ease the counting. Whether by 2s, 10s, 20s, or even 50s, counting stitches in groups is significantly easier when you start getting into higher numbers. Pattern designers will also use this technique when instructing knitters to repeat a series of stitches multiple times throughout the row or round. It's simpler to keep track of your place and catch errors if each "repeat" is placed between stitch markers.

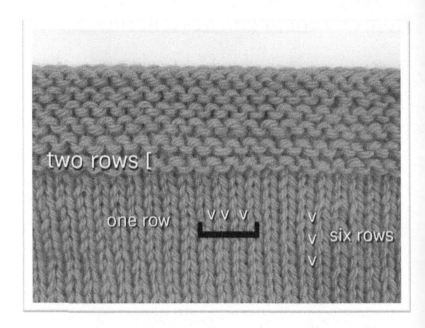

two rows [

one row   v v v

v
v six rows
v

Counting rows can be a bit trickier depending on the type of stitches being worked. Stockinette is straightforward; count the number of V's from bottom to top and stop just under the needles (the stitches on the needles haven't been worked yet, they don't count!)! Garter stitch, on the other hand, if you're counting individual ridges, then you should be counting by 2s. Each ridge in the garter stitch is comprised of 2 rows, not one. Slipped stitches also count for two rows, though usually they are accompanied by regular stitches within the row. Lace can be even more difficult to track rows without a chart to follow, row counter, or tick marks on a piece of paper so that if you put your knitting down and come back, you'll still know where in the pattern to pick up again.

Am I too young/old to learn to knit?

You are never "too old" to learn something new; in fact, adults tend to pick up new skills faster than children (languages being an exception). In the knitting community, the "golden age" for teaching children to knit is when they're about 7 or 8 years old. If you're older than 7, then you can learn to knit! There is a stigma floating around that most knitters are elderly, retired women making afghans and itchy sweaters. Perhaps this was due to attitude shifts in the 1960s and 1970s towards the older generations. It could have also been due to the decreased need for hand knit items as machine knitted products became faster and cheaper to produce. Whatever the case may be, the knitting community is an open and welcoming one, with many who are happy to pass on their skills to beginners of all ages.

What's the easiest thing for a beginner to knit?

Many, many beginning knitters start with a garter stitch scarf. It's simple enough; after you cast-on, you work the knit stitch repeatedly until it's long enough, or you feel comfortable moving on to something more challenging. If you fall into the latter category, or a third category (i.e., "I got bored and moved on"), then a good starting pattern is a dishcloth, such as Gramma's Favorite (www.ravelry.com/patterns/library/grandmothers-favorite). It is an ideal beginner project for several reasons. There are a distinct beginning and end where scarves can feel like an endless slog, which may discourage new knitters. A dishcloth knits up quickly, so the knitter feels accomplished sooner. A pattern like this one includes both increase and decrease stitches.

How can I find a yarn store or knitting classes near me?

Ravelry.com, mentioned several times in earlier chapters, has a fantastic feature that can help you locate your very own Local Yarn Shop (LYS). If you visit www.ravelry.com/yarns there is a search box that will allow you to input your City (and State or Country as applicable) and show you what's available nearby. Google and Yelp can also provide lists of shops; however, the Ravelry list will be catered to knitters and exclude large craft chains such as Michael's, Joann's, and Hobby Lobby.

Needle FAQs

Can I knit socks with 2 needles?

Yes! *Knit Your Socks On Straight* by Alice Curtis is an excellent resource for knitting socks on straight needles. Her pattern titled "Your First Pair of Socks" is knit in worsted weight on US size 6 needles, both standard beginner sizes for yarn and needles. Knitting socks flat (on straight needles) will involve either grafting or sewing the socks into a tube, which is something to keep in mind when deciding on a pattern. Additionally, there is a technique for knitting in the round that utilizes two sets of circular needles as if they are two long, flexible DPNs. There are many videos available online demonstrating this technique as well. Two circular needle sets, magic loop, or DPNs are all methods where the sock is knit as a tube, and generally, seaming is not required.

What kind of material should my needles be?

Needles, like yarn, can come in a variety of different materials. Bamboo, metal, acrylic, wood, and antique pairs of needles were made of bone or ivory. The choice of material does ultimately come down to personal preference. Metal is both familiar and inexpensive, not to mention the most durable. Acrylic and bamboo both have slight flexibility to them, which some knitters enjoy. Wood and bamboo feel warm in a knitter's hands almost instantly, which can be more comfortable for some people. Wood, however, is quite brittle, and wooden needles can break easily. Bamboo and acrylic are both a bit stronger than wood but still subject to more breaks than metal. When it comes to working with different yarn types, bamboo tends to be less slippery than metal, wood, or acrylic, and this can be preferable if you manage to drop stitches easily.

What are good needles for beginners?

US size 6 or 7 needles are excellent starting sizes for beginners as these sizes can achieve gauge in DK weight, worsted weight, and Aran weight yarn easily. The choice of circular or straight needles for a first pair is up to the knitter; however, circular needles are quite popular as they can knit in the round and flat. Straight needles can only knit flat. DPNs are not recommended for the first set of needles, but once a new knitter is more comfortable with the basics, DPNs are a good next level up.

Why are some needle tips pointier than others?

Needle tip sharpness comes down to personal preference, like the materials and sizes, but there are cases where a blunt needle may be more preferred than a sharp one, or vice versa. The heavier the yarn's weight, the more a blunt needle is generally favored so as not to "split the plies" (which means to stick the needle through the yarn itself). A needle with a sharper tip is good when knitting socks, lace, or anything with a smaller thread. Blunt tips may have trouble grabbing the stitches where sharp tips will reach for them with pin-point accuracy. Care should be taken, though, with sharp-tipped needles as even with the smaller yarn, it is still easy to split the plies if you're not watching closely.

What are interchangeable needles?

Several companies make a variety of circular needles known as "interchangeable." It is where the needles themselves are screwed onto the cables and can be removed or swapped with another size. There are many benefits to this type of set, including the ability to change needle sizes on the same project without having to knit from one set to another while changing sizes (frequently, ribbing is knit in a smaller size than the rest of a project). Additionally, if you need to put a project on hold and use the same size needles for something else, you can remove the needles and replace them with stoppers to keep the stitches from sliding off the cable. No more fussing with scrap yarn or stitch holders! Interchangeable needle sets come in a variety of sizes, though typically, they are the most common. It isn't easy to find interchangeable needles in specialty sizes such as US 00 or US 50, and usually, these are sold separately from other sets. Another benefit to interchangeable needle sets is that you can also purchase connector pieces to make the cables long enough for any project, including blankets. There might not be an 80-inch pair of circular needles on the market, but with the right set of interchangeable needles, you can fashion one for yourself!

Do square knitting needles exist?

Yes! Some knitters swear by them, saying the square needles are more ergonomic and easier on their hands than traditional round needles. In most cases, only the shaft of the needle is square; the tip itself (and cable if we're talking about circular needles) is still round and tapers into the square. The corners of the square needles are not sharp enough to hurt or bother your fingers while you're working with them and have an additional tactile feeling for those who like more sensory input. Non-round needles are still a relatively new addition to the knitting world. They first entered the market in 2006 when a company called Kollage began selling them, and they started to gather a cult following. From there, other companies, such as Louet, Knitter's Pride, and Knit picks, all began selling their versions of the square needles.

Yarn FAQs

What size needles and how much yarn do I need?

The short answer is it depends. Both the needle size and yarn amount depend on which weight you are going to use. "Weight" in this case refers to the thickness of the yarn rather than how heavy it is. Below is a table that shows general needle size, yarn weight, and amount ratios for a pair of adult crew-length socks.

Needle Size	Yarn Weight	Yarn Amount
US 00-2	Fingering	≤ 400 yards
US 1-3	Sport	≤ 400 yards
US 3-5	DK	≤ 300 yards
US 4-7	Worsted	≤ 300 yards
US 6-9	Bulky	≤ 200 yards

Actual numbers may vary depending on your gauge, the pattern used, and the overall sock length. Ankle socks require significantly less yarn than crew length, but knee-high socks require much more. Knitters with a tight gauge may find they need more thread than knitters who knit with a looser gauge as well.

How can I tell what weight a yarn is?

If you're in a store, the label on the yarn itself will tell you, and if you're shopping online, the individual listing should say the yarn's weight. Some online retailers will also sort their inventory by weight, which is helpful.

What if the yarn label doesn't say the weight?

Most of the yarn in chain craft stores will have the yarn weight on the label; however, there are occasions where the weight isn't on the label. It happens more often in specialty yarn shops or on yarn from high-end dyers. In this instance, there are two things you can look at on the label to get an idea of the yarn weight. The first is the actual weight in grams. In the above example, the fingering weight yarn has 231 yards per 50 grams, while the worsted weight only has 110 yards per 50 grams. They weigh the same, but one has significantly less yardage than the other; that's the "heavier" weight yarn.

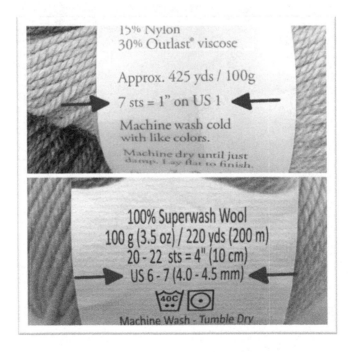

The other way to tell what the yarn weight is by looking at the label is the recommended needle size. Fingering weight yarn will use smaller needles, for example, than a DK or worsted weight yarn. While the table from the "What size needles and how much yarn do I need" question is a generalization of the ratio between needle and yarn sizes, the same idea can be applied when determining the thread's weight based on the label.

How many skeins of yarn should I buy to knit socks?

It gets tricky because "skein" is not a standard measurement unit for yarn; it's usually a reference to how the yarn is wound. See below for examples of different ways yarn can be wound.

Skeins can vary in yardage by both weight and brand. Two 400-yard skeins are twice as much yarn as two 200-yard skeins. The best thing to do is read the labels of yarn you like, see how many yards (or meters) are listed, and compare that to what your pattern says it needs.

Cake   Skein

Ball   Hank

Can I knit socks with acrylic or cotton yarn?

Cotton and acrylic yarns benefit from being machine washable, which makes them attractive to many knitters. There are a couple of downsides to consider when deciding whether to use acrylic or cotton yarn for socks. The first issue is that acrylic yarn not as breathable as wool. Human feet can sweat up to a liter a day, and the polyester of acrylic yarn does not wick the moisture away. Cotton yarn is more breathable but lacks the elasticity that wool yarn has, which can cause socks to stretch out and lose shape over time. If stretched-out socks or sweaty feet are not going to be an issue, then socks can absolutely be made from cotton and acrylic yarns.

What type of yarn is best for knitting socks?

The "best" is truly "whatever works for you." Many knitters prefer to knit in fingering weight yarn that is a nylon blend (typically with wool) to knit their socks, but that does not mean you MUST choose the same! If you want to knit worsted weight socks in Alpaca because that feels best for you, then knit yourself those Alpaca socks. Nylon blends will hold up better over many wears, but if you don't enjoy knitting with that type of yarn, use a type you do enjoy. In terms of human history, nylon has only been around for a short time, and people were knitting socks for centuries without it.

Why is wool yarn so expensive?

Acrylic yarn is made from spun and dyed polyester, a synthetic fiber that is both cheap and easy to make (relatively speaking) in large quantities. The savings in both time, effort, and cost are passed onto the consumer. Wool yarn, on the other hand, must be sourced from a farm, sheared from the sheep, carded or combed (to remove what is colloquially known as "veg matter" and dirt from the fleece), then spun into a single ply, spun again into multiple plies, and dyed. Wool yarns can be produced in large batches, much like acrylic, and some mills can control their entire supply chain to help reduce costs. If you are knitting on a budget, the large chain craft stores will be your best source of inexpensive acrylic and wool yarn. Online brands that carry less expensive lines of thread also include Knit Picks (www.knitpicks.com) and Cascade Yarns (www.cascadeyarns.com).

Is it normal for my hand-knit socks to bleed color when I wash them?

Yes, depending on the type of yarn, the dye method used, and the color, it is highly likely that some color bleeding will occur during a wash. Don't worry, though; you won't lose all your color! If you're washing your socks by themselves, there's really no harm done, though you do want to be careful if you're washing multiple pairs of socks together. Black, red, and pink yarn dyes are notorious for bleeding in the wash, and you may want to wash those colors separately if possible. Color catchers are available to purchase at various stores, and they serve to soak up any loose dye in the water before it can get to your lighter-colored socks.

What is the best way to wind yarn?

If your yarn came in a ball, cake, or skein, then you can knit directly from it as it is. If your thread came to you in a hank (a twist of yarn), you'd need to wind it first before you can knit with it. The easiest method to wind yarn is with a ball winder (which is a misnomer, it winds your yarn into cakes!) and a swift. A swift expands like an umbrella and spins like a carousel. It allows you to unwind your hank, snip the small ties that keep the yarn from getting tangled, and pull (almost) continuously to wind the yarn. If you do not have access to a ball winder and swift, you can get creative! Winding yarn into balls is often seen in movies and TV shows with two people, where one is holding the unwound hank, and the other is winding the yarn into a ball. Knitters have also gotten creative and used the backs of two chairs or even their own feet to hold the thread as they wind!

About the Expert

Jeanne Torrey lives near Baltimore, Maryland, with her three kids, college BFF, and tuxedo cat. She has been knitting since 2010 and has knit more than 30 pairs of socks. You can find her on Ravelry.com under the username KnitsaTrap. When she's not knitting, Jeanne enjoys sewing, writing, and video games. She also practices the martial arts of Tae-Kwon-Do (currently a 2nd-degree black belt), Eskrima (green sash, Cacoy Doces Pares) and has recently taken up violin lessons. Honorable mentions go to Jeanne's longtime friends: Lyndsay, who had the patience to teach her (twice) how to knit, and Jessica, who provides incredible moral support. This book is dedicated to her family and to Melissa, who insists she won't be able to knit socks. Yes, you can, Melissa!

HowExpert publishes quick 'how to' guides on all topics from A to Z by everyday experts. Visit HowExpert.com to learn more.

Recommended Resources

- HowExpert.com – Quick 'How To' Guides on All Topics from A to Z by Everyday Experts.
- HowExpert.com/free – Free HowExpert Email Newsletter.
- HowExpert.com/books – HowExpert Books
- HowExpert.com/courses – HowExpert Courses
- HowExpert.com/clothing – HowExpert Clothing
- HowExpert.com/membership – HowExpert Membership Site
- HowExpert.com/affiliates – HowExpert Affiliate Program
- HowExpert.com/jobs – HowExpert Jobs
- HowExpert.com/writers – Write About Your #1 Passion/Knowledge/Expertise & Become a HowExpert Author.
- HowExpert.com/resources – Additional HowExpert Recommended Resources
- YouTube.com/HowExpert – Subscribe to HowExpert YouTube.
- Instagram.com/HowExpert – Follow HowExpert on Instagram.
- Facebook.com/HowExpert – Follow HowExpert on Facebook.

Made in the USA
Monee, IL
21 January 2023

25865077R00132